GOOD DIRT

Kingdomtide

A Devotional for the Spiritual Formation of Families

Lacy Finn Borgo & Ben Barczi

Printed in the United States of America.

First Printing, 2014.

ISBN-10: 1499642547

ISBN-13: 978-1499642544

Lacy dedicates this book
to Aidan, Anwen, Sean, Dallas and Kaylie:
Thank you for teaching me to be like Jesus.

Ben dedicates this book
to the Fitler, Gies, Laymon, Steckling, and Weyel families:
Thank you for including me in the stories and rhythms of your homes.

CONTENTS

. . . .

Appendices

SERIES INTRODUCTION

··

Dirt Matters

Pete Collum is my (Lacy's) grandfather and at his very core he is a gardener. Wherever he has lived, he has planted something. When he and my grandmother, Lillian, lived in a dilapidated building that used to be their deli grocery store, surrounded by machine shops and oil field workers, he found tiny patches of dirt and planted watermelons, tomatoes and okra. Armed with a hat that had seen better days, a pocket full of seeds, and a belief in the miracle of growth he stepped into the realm of the Creator and worked. That Permian Basin dirt is full of shale and black gold, but it needs a bit of help if you hope to get squash and tomatoes. He is always puttering around outside, burring scraps, propping up plants, watering, irrigating, and weeding.

It has been said that nature is the first book we read about God. As created beings on a created planet we learn so much from simply looking around a bit.

As a little girl sitting on a paint can in PaPete's garden, I watched him. I saw how the presence of water can change even the look of a plant in a matter of minutes. I saw that if you pull weeds when they are small, their roots are smaller so require less elbow grease to remove. I saw that the row where we buried garden scraps months before had the healthiest plants. I tasted warm watermelon still on the vine, sweetened by the sun.

While listening to Dallas Willard at the Renovaré Institute for Spiritual Formation, this scene came back to me. Spiritual formation has remarkable similarities to garden living and tending. Of course, as parents of young persons and children of God, we live in the garden we tend. The metaphor of the garden can help us enter spiritual formation more fully. And, since we are seasonal creatures born on a seasonal planet, it made perfect sense to me to engage in the Seasons of the Church as part of family spiritual formation. Knowing right away I was in over my head, I enlisted a fellow student, Ben Barczi, for help. He's a spiritual formation pastor who lives the Seasons of the Church. We brainstormed this idea and wrote *Good Dirt* together. It is our desire that our voices are heard in harmony and so many of the narratives are written in first person.

Spiritual Formation: Tending Your Garden

God has given us both the seed of our own souls and the souls of the little ones that live in our homes and leave their gum on the table. Our job is to till, plant, water, and weed, doing what we can to make our family soil rich in the love of God. In the same way that gardens need constant care, so do souls, both little and big ones. This devotional is designed to help you work in the garden of your family throughout your day. It is designed to help you set a daily rhythm of tilling, planting, watering and weeding.

» **Till:** Greet the day with prayer, such as, "Good Morning Master Gardener. We will need your help today. And thanks for the rain." Perhaps praying together at the breakfast table will work for your family, or snuggled together in bed before the day begins.

» **Plant:** Meditate on scripture, for the good seed of God is his Word. There is nothing better for the little and big souls in families. Read it aloud. Have your newest family reader read, or your oldest, or boldest. What an honor to speak these words of life. If everyone is willing, read it twice. Read it slow. Let it seep in—let it leach the life-giving vitamins and minerals into the family. Let it feed these souls.

» **Water:** Reflect. We've got to have water. Water not only hydrates, it also carries vitamins and minerals to where they are needed. Reflection, like water, is a carrier: it carries the truths of scripture straight to the center of the heart where they can do the most good.

» **Weed:** Examine. If weeds are not pulled in a garden they will choke out all life. That is the harsh truth of gardens and people. Even preschoolers can examine their days. They know very well when they have obeyed and when they have not. Just before bedtime is the perfect time to examine the day, to ask the questions: what in my day today was life giving, and what was not? How did I walk in the light today, or not? Ending with prayer entrusts the process of growth into God's hands:

> *Lord, we brings these things to you. Glory to Father and to the Son and to the Holy Spirit, as it was in the beginning, is now, and will be forever, Amen.*

Suggested Rhythms for Daily Garden Care:

» **Rhythm #1:**
AM (Breakfast): Till and Plant
Noon: Water
PM (Dinner): Plant and Water
Bedtime: Weed

» **Rhythm #2:**
AM (Breakfast) Till
Noon: Plant
PM (Dinner): Plant, Water
Bedtime: Weed

» **Rhythm #3:**
AM (Breakfast): Till
Noon: Plant, Water
PM (Dinner): Plant, Water
Bedtime: Weed

» **Rhythm #4**
AM (Breakfast): Till, Plant
Noon: Take a pause to thank the Giver of Growth.
PM (Dinner): Plant, Water
Bedtime: Weed

There are many different combinations that can be used for daily garden care. Between waking up and going to bed, just be sure to till, plant, water, and weed, as a family. As flexible as this can be, it is very helpful to establish a rhythm, the same time to do the same thing day after day. Daily rhythms evoke a sense of security. Rhythms give families a knowing expectation of what is to come.

Spiritual formation has four major elements: your life, spiritual disciplines, Jesus' life, and the Holy Spirit. We have woven these elements into the daily and monthly rhythms. The first element of spiritual formation is **your life.** As a smart-mouthed teen of the '80s I often quipped at friends, "Get a Life." But the truth of the matter is we have a life. We may not love it, and it may not be exactly what we wish, but I've got a life, and you've got a life. You've got a garden. In your garden there is rain, sleet, drought, squirrels, and perhaps on some days too much manure. In your garden you have sprouts; the tiny plants God has given you, the ones that look to you for food and water. The tiny plants that beg to stay up past their bed time, the ones that argue with their sister. The ones that beg for candy in the checkout line, and give away their toys to a friend who has little. You have the shade trees of a good friends, or supportive family. Maybe you've even got a plant or two that would do better in another garden, but you keep it because it's just too hard to change and love rightly. And to keep it real, you've also got weeds; maybe they are sins that seek to choke you or your sprouts.

We are formed by our environment, for good or bad. I spent some of my earliest and best years in my grandparents' old deli in the middle of oil field workers and welding shops. I was formed by this environment. As a result, I learned hospitality: my grandparents welcomed each person who entered their deli. Race or gender had no bearing on how they treated people. I learned responsibility; they gave me jobs to do and the value that came from them depending on my job. I also picked up a colorful vocabulary. I didn't know "shit" was not universally accepted vocabulary until I began attending a Christian School. I did learn fast though.

The second element for spiritual formation is **spiritual practices or disciplines**. These are tools that work life and light into our gardens. Some tools we have used before. They are tried and true. For example, I grew up in a Southern Baptist church, and Southern Baptists read their Bibles and journal. These are good tools to connect us with the Life Changer.

Sometimes we need to change out even our favorite tools. After a while, journaling became a place for me to judge others and whine about my life. So I took a good ten years off journaling. Only recently have I started again, and this time, I only write what I hear God saying to me. The old tool needed retooling, but throw a good tool away? Never. But if the ground has changed, or your soul has had more rain, or even drought, that may call for a new tool.

Spiritual disciplines or practices open the space for God to feed and shape your garden. For example, praying puts you in contact with the Master Gardener. Confession is an exercise in weed pulling. Simplicity keeps us from planting more than our soil can sustain. These habits form us. In this devotional we will engage in many of these life-forming habits. We will practice twelve classic practices Richard Foster writes about in his book *Celebration of Discipline*, as well as some others.

The third element for spiritual formation in families is **Jesus' life**. Dallas Willard describes the work of spiritual formation as taking on, bit by bit, Jesus' ideas and images about God, life, and the world, so that they gradually replace our own. We want to be able to look at our everyday life—the dishes, the noisy neighbor, the grubby kids, the mailman, our boss—and be able to see them and live with them in light of the loving, good God that Jesus knew.

The primary place we get instruction and guidance on the with-God life is Jesus. "No one has seen the Father," Jesus' best friend, John, wrote. Now there's a problem—how can we do life with someone no one has ever seen? But John knew the solution, because he snuggled up to him at the Last Supper: "This one-of-a-kind God-Expression, who exists at the very heart of the Father, has made him plain as day." (John 1:18, *The Message*)

It is in the one-of-a-kind life and teaching of Jesus that we get the help we need to replace our unhelpful images of God and life with the ones that shaped the mind of Jesus. We watch him talk to God, rejoice in God, weep with God, listen to God, and lead others to God. And, most of all, we see him show God's love: eating with sinners, touching the untouchables, and laying down his life with arms stretched out to embrace the world. That's why in *Good Dirt* we journey with Jesus through the Gospels. In the recorded memories of the disciples, the research of Luke, the reminiscing of Peter handed to Mark, we have an expression of the life of Jesus that takes our breath away—if we will pay attention!

So we need to meditate on and study Jesus' life. Both of those terms get a bad rap, because they sound either mystical or boring. But kids do both naturally. Meditation is just turning over and over an idea, imaginatively, entering it and playing with it and seeing what it means and how it works. Kids meditate on ladybugs and anthills and dogs' tails and sand between their fingers. And study—far from being boring work done in a hushed library—is keeping our attention on something so that it becomes part of us. Kids study their favorite super hero, they study mom and dad, they study cartoons and they study their older siblings. ("He's copying me!" Yes, exactly—the child is watching and absorbing mannerisms until they think and act just like the one they've studied.) So studying and meditating aren't as much of a stretch as we'd think, and the Gospels make wonderful material to study Jesus and his one-of-a-kind God-Expression life.

We also get help in journeying with Jesus from the Seasons of the Church. In this devotional we are immersing our lives in the life of Jesus by celebrating the Seasons of the Church. Another way to say it is that we are marking our lives by the life of Jesus. The Christian Church began formally celebrating Easter as early as 325AD, and even before that Israel had seasons of fasting and feasting to mark their story with God throughout the ages. There is a great cloud of witnesses that have gone before us.

The seasons follow a pattern of preparation, celebration, and then living out what we have prepared for and celebrated. In Advent we prepare for God with us, at Christmastide we celebrate God with us, and during Epiphany we step into a life with God. In Lent we prepare for our own death and the death of Jesus, at Eastertide we celebrate that he died, is risen and us with him, and during Pentecost and Kingdomtide we live out his resurrection and ours. We are meant to live seasonally. Who can feast all the time without becoming a glutton? Who can fast or mourn all the time without losing their mind? When our days lose the gift of thankfulness and celebration we become a depressed and dying people. As the physical seasons set the rhythm of the earth, so the church season can set our rhythm to the rhythm of Christ.

There are seven main seasons of the church. The great diversity of our Christian traditions means that some seasons are named slightly differently and some dates are variable, but this is the overall, middle of the road, happy medium, church calendar.

Seasons of the Church

» **Advent:** Four weeks. Color: Royal Blue

» **Christmastide:** Twelve days, until the eve of Epiphany on January 5. Color: White

» **Epiphany:** Eight weeks, give or take a few weeks depending on when Easter falls; plus a little at the beginning and a little at the end to get us to Ash Wednesday for Lent. Color: Green

» **Lent:** Five weeks, plus a little at the beginning and a full week of Holy Week. Color: Purple

» **Eastertide:** Seven weeks up to Pentecost Sunday. Color: White

» **Pentecost:** One week, which is included as the last week of Eastertide. Color: Red

» **Kingdomtide:** Twenty-eight weeks, give or take a few weeks depending on when Easter falls. Color: Green

Do all these dates sound confusing? No worries, we put a calendar of specific dates at the end of the book. In time these seasons will become second nature.

How to Make a Seasons of the Church Calendar

First, a confession. The first three times I made one of these it was a disaster, mostly because I'm an adult. In my first attempt, I couldn't make myself label the seasons counter-clockwise. The calendar moves counterclockwise to remind us that we live countercultural to the world and its systems of destruction and death. However, in my forty years on this planet, I have learned that everything moves clockwise; going against the grain requires more thinking than I can summon. Funny thing though, my seven-year-old and ten-year-old pulled it off. "It's easy, Mom," they said. Likely story. In my second attempt, I spelled Epiphany wrong, in permanent marker. My Southern Baptist roots betray me. Who ever heard of Epiphany in the first place? And for my final attempt, I couldn't get the dashes evenly spaced to mark the weeks. There were rulers, protractors, and a host of other instruments I hadn't used since high school geometry. Once again counseled by people not even of driving age, I realized I was letting this calendar use me. Got it. So I stepped back and let the kids make it. It's great and it's attached to our fridge.

> **Materials:** poster board, pencils, permanent markers, rulers (only one and no more tools) crayons, 1 brass brad

> 1. This calendar will look very much like an analog clock. Cut a large circle (as large as you want your calendar to be) out of the poster board.

> 2. Divide the calendar into seven sections, like a pie graph. Take a look at the seasons listed above, estimate that, for example, Kingdomtide will need the most space because it has the most weeks. Pentecost and Christmastide will have tiny spaces. Remember: the seasons go in counter-clockwise order. For example: make a space for Advent, then move to the left for Christmastide, etc. If you get stuck ask your kid for help.

> 3. Within each season make "dashes," like the five minute marks on an analog clock, to represent the weeks contained in each season.

> 4. Write the name of the season on its space. Fill in the season space with its color (see the list above).

> 5. Cut out an arrow from the poster board. Use the brass brad to attach it to the middle of the calendar.

Optional Additions: Put a star on Christmastide, and a Cross on the first week of Eastertide. Invite or encourage your children to research the history and tradition of the seasons and write a list of their symbols in their space. Decorate the house with these symbols when their season comes around. A friend of mine has wind chimes hanging over her kitchen bar, and changes the items on the chime as the seasons change. We change the items on our mantle. All of this is not to make us consumers; in fact it's more fun to make some of these items. Like the icons used in the Orthodox Christian tradition, they are open windows into the life of Jesus. They remind us that we mark our lives by his life.

The fourth element for spiritual formation in families is the **Holy Spirit**. We can prepare the dirt, we can water and weed, but we don't make things grow. We have no control over sun, rain or wind. We aren't even in charge of the seed we are given: we do not choose our talents and inclinations. The Holy Spirit gives the seed. The Holy Spirit makes things grow. We do not control the outcomes, and it's a good thing: having control is dangerous for us. Getting just what we want and hope can make us hell to live around. Having complete control leads us to cast judgment on others. Even thinking we should have control can make us a mess. Think of the parents of children who have struggled or self-destructed? Parents who think they are in control beat themselves up for doing it wrong. They carry the crushing burdens of "should have", "would have" and "could have." How wonderful that we have the Holy Spirit working on our behalf. We learn to do our part and trust the Holy Spirit for the rest.

Everybody's Got Parts

In a garden, plants have parts. And those parts have different jobs and have different needs. People have parts too. The most obvious part we have is our body.

We were only one song into Sunday morning when Julie began to lead them in. All seven preschoolers followed dutifully behind our children's director to the front row. The switch to modern worship music hasn't been easy for most of the church. The hymns are the songs of their faith, their struggles, but graciously, they sing. They don't clap, but they do sing. And so did the preschoolers. They belted out those tunes like they had sung them all their lives. First they worshiped with their mouths. Then a few began to sway; they started clapping their hands; a few even let loose a full-body jig. As someone who is with children on a regular basis this was no surprise to me. I know they can't hide joy in their bodies. But I was surprised at how their transparency spread through the church. While the congregation watched the children, who frankly couldn't be ignored, folks began to smile, and then clap, and even—dare I say it?—sway. "Is this how the children will lead us?" I thought. They will lead us to worship God with our whole selves.

Children, like adults, have parts. Children have a body, a mind, a spirit, a soul, and a village. Dallas Willard in *Renovation of the Heart* calls "village" a social context.[1] This refers to the folks that influence us as well as the ones we influence. This village does shape us. Jesus mentions each of these parts as he gives us the For Dummies version of the Ten Commandments, "Love the Lord you God with all your heart [spirit], and with all your soul [soul] and with all your mind, [mind], with all your strength [body]…, and love your neighbor [village or social context] as yourself." (Mark 12:30-31) When we talk about spiritual formation we are talking about all these parts being invited into relationship with God. All of these parts come to live in the kingdom of God.

Our children's bodies which we lovingly wash and feed are created by God and created like all their other parts to be in relationship with him. As a born Southern Baptist, who is currently Nazarene, but loves everything Catholic, I have to say that the best part of the twelve days of Christmastide is meditating on the Incarnation. God himself enters creation in a human body, a real human body. The Gnostics and the Church Fathers went round and round over this. Did Jesus have a real human body, you know, one that got the flu and threw up, one that had body odor, one that danced when he felt joy, one that wept when he felt sadness? Our Church Fathers fought the good fight to say that, yes, he had and still does have a real body. For us, the incarnation, Jesus in a real human body, means that our bodies are redeemable. God's intention for bodies is goodness. He declares it so in Genesis 1, and who am I to contradict that?

Children cannot hide the condition of their spirit, mind or emotion behind their bodies. Adults can, but children simply cannot pull it off. This is a major advantage for children as we think about how they live their lives with Jesus. When they are sad, sadness leaks out of their eyes; it is shown in their bodies. Adults, on the other hand, have been taught when these emotions are appropriate and when they are not, and we are often trained to deny even having these emotions.

Equally so, children can't hide their thoughts. During sharing time in thousands of elementary schools across America, children are sharing what they are thinking about. Mostly what they have to say is not even loosely related to the topic at hand, but it's on their mind and they have a desire to tell someone.

---

1 For a full and frankly fantastic teaching on the parts of the person and how they are formed into Christlikeness check out *Renovation of the Heart* by Dallas Willard.

The desire to share comes from the divinely inspired, very human, desire to be known—for the hidden parts of us to be known and accepted by another. Children in healthy environments have no inclination that hidden parts should stay hidden or that any thought they have wouldn't be welcomed by any hearers.

Rightly ordered the spirit is the command center of the person. "Out of the heart the mouth speaks," the scriptures remind us. Jesus refers to it in his simple version of the commandments. "Love the Lord your God with all your heart and soul." However our spirit is formed so goes the rest of the person. Interestingly enough educational sciences are discovering that we are formed by experiences more than we are formed by formal teaching. Churches over the last hundred or so years have invested truck loads of resources in education of children and I think if we look back we might question the results. At least in the last twenty years we have seen a mass exit of young people from the church. Could one of the reasons be that formal teaching does not actually hold the weight in formation that experience does? Could it be that the experiences of formation offered by the secular world outweighed the formal teaching of Christian education?

The key to the power in experience over formal teaching lies in our wiring. We are created to take in information through our five senses, engaging all the parts of our person. What the body experiences is taken into the spirit, and like capillary action moves to all our other parts and formation happens. Living a life with God is not confined to an intellectual understanding. All the parts of the person live a life with God. Everything. He came to redeem it all. That's the good news. We get a whole, not partial, salvation.

Seasonal Fun

The seasonal fun section contains opportunities to mark our lives by the life of Jesus. In this section there are many activities, crafts, celebrations, suggestions, songs, harebrained ideas, and general chances for fun. Please, do not set out to do them all. Do not. You will make yourself and your family crazy. Instead, during each season choose a few, the ones that are suited to where you are in your family, for example toddlers versus teenagers. Next year choose some that you didn't do the previous year.

Marking your life by the life of Jesus for one year will change you for sure, but imagine with me the difference it will make marking it each year for the rest of your life on earth. Imagine. Imagine the difference it will make in the lives of your children as you bring them into the knowledge and relationship with Jesus first through observation and participation in the rituals of the season and then when they are old enough reading through the gospels.

Seasonal Fun is where we live out in our bodies the marking of our lives by Jesus' life. For example, the celebration of Eastertide has its chance to work resurrection into our minds through bodies as we have a mini-celebration every Sunday during the seven weeks of the season.

Family Structures

In this devotional we reference moms and dads and children. But rest assured, if your family structure doesn't look like this, this is still for you! Today's family structures are varied and those structures too are included in Jesus' invitation to the kingdom. Our intimate communities often include friends, and extended family members. From my point of view this is wonderful. When we use the word "family" in this devotional we are including those in your intimate community, those living and eating with you.

Family Listening

As a people we're pretty good about talking, and telling. We've got stories to tell and opinions to convey. However, part of the relationship process with each other and with God is listening. In this devotional we will encourage you to practice listening. Good listening, complete with eye contact, affirmations, and a zippered lip. Every day you will be challenged to listen to God, and to discern with one another his voice and message. We often think of hearing from God as an other-worldly, only-when-smoke-is-involved matter, but that couldn't be farther from the truth. Listening to God, like listening to others, is a product of experience. You know your mother's voice because you have heard it over and over again. When we hear a voice we think is God's we check it against 1 Corinthians 13. Was the voice patient and kind? How about gentle and generous? If so that was God and we fix that experience in our souls. Each additional experience we have with God's voice builds our confidence. After a while it won't be long before we don't even have to look we know it was God who spoke, because we've heard him before.[2]

And What about the Littlest People?

This is a family rhythm, and because families can range in ages, we've aimed at the middle. Every aspect—Till, Plant, Water and Weed—can be "rounded" up or down. "Rounding" up is rarely a problem, but what about the littlest members of our family? How does this nurture the preschool people?

These little interactive sponges have all senses on go! The real value of ritual, which involves so many of the senses, is spent on the little ones. Each night during Advent as the candles are lit, their minds are drinking in that 'light dispels darkness' and 'the One who is celebrated is the light.' The regularity of ritual teaches far more than wordy explanations. The Seasonal Fun section is the main teaching tool for small children. In living the seasons and reading the scriptures year after year, an essential foundation is being built on the Rock. They are listening when the scriptures are being read. Furthermore, they understand far more than we realize. It is not that we, the knowing adults, have to introduce them to God. They very recently were knitted together in their mother's womb. They know the Knitter. However, at their developmental stage they lack the language to express what they know. It is, nevertheless, up to us, their parents, to teach them the language, and to teach them what a relationship with God looks like on this earth.

---

2 Dallas Willard's book *Hearing God: Developing a Conversational Relationship with God,* has been instrumental in deepening our knowledge and practice of hearing and discerning the voice of God.

KINGDOMTIDE

During the summer these words bellow from the porches and couches of millions of homes in America: "I'm bored." Every kid in the free world, having prayed fervently for school to end, is now proclaiming that the day of perpetual boredom is here.

In our culture the tendency is to fill up the summer with camps, classes, and distractions of every shape and color. What would happen if we halted our planning and pondered the wisdom of Kingdomtide, or as it is traditionally called, Ordinary Time?

What is ordinary? Oatmeal for breakfast is ordinary. Laundry, the sun coming up, rain, reading to my kids, mowing the lawn, feeding the chickens, making the bed, napping on Sunday—all ordinary. Without these ordinary actions, our lives lose a sense of rhythm. In fact, without the ordinary we don't grow, not physically or spiritually. There is nothing fancy or fabulous about a meal of beans and cornbread, except that it sustains our bodies, and thousands of people eat it every day. It is an ordinary meal that does extraordinary things. The fact that the sun comes up every day is an ordinary event most of us ignore, but without it nothing could live. Jesus was so fond of teaching out of ordinariness, over dinner, in a wheat field. He taught the foundational truths of the universe out of an ordinary body, using ordinary words, to ordinary people.

For six seasons now, we (Lacy and Ben and you!) have looked forward and backward; we've celebrated and mourned. Now, during Kingdomtide, we settle in: we find our stride. For 29 full weeks we all have the chance to establish a family rhythm that will grow us and ours.

Many families practice the spiritual discipline of vacation during Kingdomtide, but for most vacation is just one week in the midst of 29 weeks of ordinary. The other 28 weeks are the lazy days of summer, complete with marshmallow roasting, watermelon seed spitting, and bike riding. We intermingle these sorts of activities with the open space of unscheduled time. For children and for their adults, this is the season of rhythms to build a life on.

We might think that the rhythms and lessons of ordinariness will just meander their way into our homes—and maybe this used to be so. But in a culture built on desire and distraction, ordinariness is endangered. Building a life on the rhythms of ordinariness takes intention and attention. We will have to intend to walk slowly with our kids to the mailbox while stopping and looking at every bug that passes by. We will have to think to grab a stick and play pirate with the neighbor kids. We will have to watch for the teachable moments of forgiveness when siblings quarrel. We will have to be determined to teach the time-honored skill of pancake flipping infused with thankfulness. We will need to plan to lie in the backyard and teach the names of the constellations, or make up our own. During the ordinary routines of eating and sleeping, rest and work, moments will slip up on us that are golden for teaching the way of Jesus. It is our job to lessen the distractions so we will recognize these moments when they come our way. If we do this, our TV's will grow dusty, our schedule will look empty, and when people ask what our big plans are for the summer, we will say with a knowing smile, "Oh nothing, absolutely nothing."

Seasonal Fun

Warning: All or most of these will be ordinary.

» Just Say No: For one summer, say no to as many obligations as possible. Play outside as a family daily, perhaps, after work in the cool of the evening. It's great stress relief.

» Go camping, even if it's in your backyard, which actually can be the best way. (The bathroom's closer.)

» Reread the section in this booklet on Family Rhythm. Plan a way to make it a part of your family's day.

» Make popsicles.

» Collect rocks.

» Swing by your local appliance store, and ask for a refrigerator box. Then ask your children if you can help them create a fort. The adult must follow the child's instructions. Use old paint, or markers, or crayons. Don't wear your best clothes.

» Establish a family game night. Invite the neighbors.

» Refuse to use the TV/electronic gaming apparatus as a babysitter.

» Read *The Hobbit* by J.R.R. Tolkien or *The Chronicles of Narnia* by C.S. Lewis to your children.

Vacation as a Spiritual Discipline

Vacation is that rare week in the midst of summer when nothing is ordinary. We embark on an adventure with the ones we love, often as we empty our pocketbooks. As a family we've gone this route before, and it seems like every family must do it at least once, creating new bonds in the midst of overexposure to plastic animated whatzits, heatstroke, and mystery-meat burgers. But the best vacations Lacy's family has ever enjoyed have been the cheapest ones: visits to national and state parks.

Americans are very fortunate to have our national parks. Although your family may be skeptical about "nature vacations," we have had more adventures (read, "opportunities for family bonding") in national parks than anywhere else. Theme parks don't hold a candle to lunch with a grizzly in Yellowstone, or climbing the steep ladders of Mesa Verde. Both we've done, not exactly on purpose; but certainly we were bound together through our adventure and still tell the stories. Even if yours is a less-than-tent-friendly family, many parks have cabins, so the camping piece is optional.

Americans pride ourselves on our work ethic, and work is good. But no matter what route you choose, be sure to take one week—or two if you can—and vacation.

Vacation Helps:

» Hold a family meeting and discuss the options.

» If your children are older, let them in on the family vacation budget. Teaching responsible money skills can't start too soon.

» Encourage children to make their own packing list. (Be sure to check it, or you may end up at Zion National Park with a bag full of Lego bricks but no underwear!)

Where do I start in Kingdomtide?

The church calendar can be a tricky thing. Most prayer books and lectionaries come with a table in the back which requires an advanced degree in lunar astrophysics and liturgical history even to begin using. We've tried to avoid that in Good Dirt as much as possible, but the fact that the date of Easter slips around with the lunar cycle makes things tricky. After the season of Easter, we begin Kingdomtide (usually called Ordinary Time—as in ordinal, or numbered, because these weeks of the year are assigned numbers from 1 to 29). For ease of use, we've gone ahead and just called these weeks by what date they're closest to. So, "Week of Sunday closest to May 11" means—well, what it says: whatever Sunday is closest to May 11, that's the day to begin that week's set of readings and activities. In some years you will be skipping over some of the 29 weeks, but in other years you'll cycle back around to them, so don't worry.

Week of Sunday closest to May 18

Sunday

Till: We praise you, Father, Son and Holy Spirit! What a mystery you are! We love knowing that we have a Father, that Jesus is our God and Savior, and that your Spirit is with us always. We praise you!

Plant: John 1:1-18

Water:

» Draw it: One common symbol for the Trinity is three rings that all intersect each other (like a Venn diagram with three circles). Have each child draw this, and then in each ring, write or draw what that person is like. What is the Father like? What is the Son like? What is the Spirit like? You can use words or images.

» Apply it: How does it make you feel to know that God is Father, Son, and Spirit—that God is three persons who love each other very, very much?

Weed: Think over your day. Where did you encounter the Father today? The Son? The Spirit?

Monday

Till: God, you are always seeking our growth, working so that we can bear fruit. Feed us. Give us what we need to bring forth the delicious fruit of love, joy, and peace!

Plant: Luke 13:1-9

Water:

> »   Enter it: Today's story focuses on how God intends to grow us, so we can bear the fruit of loving him and loving others. Make the story tangible: Together water indoor or outdoor plants. As you do, think about how God is feeding and watering you.

> »   Apply it: These two stories seem unrelated, but they aren't. Jesus is pointing out that God is not in the business of chopping us down or crushing us under buildings in response to our sin. His response to our sin is to feed and water us so that we change from the inside! He responds to our fruitlessness with love. God is the good gardener! What are some ways God is feeding and watering you right now? Keep your eyes open today for God feeding and watering you.

Weed: When did God feed and water you? When did you bear good fruit? Were there times that were more fruitless? When did you feel love today? When did you give love today?

Tuesday

Till: Jesus, you love us so much! You showed us that people are more important than rules, that love is better than just not making a mistake. Help us love like you!

Plant: Luke 13:10-17

Water:

» Draw it: Draw Jesus healing the woman, with the red-faced critics looking on.

» Apply it: The leaders of the Jewish people were really trying to be good, but their idea of goodness was to avoid breaking rules. Jesus' idea of goodness was active and life-giving—to love people and help them. Today, instead of trying not to do things wrong, how could you show active love?

» Weed: What was it like focusing on love instead of rules? When do you tend to forget love and just think about avoiding mistakes? When did you give love today? When did you receive love today?

Wednesday

Till: God, your kingdom shows up in ways that look unimpressive and tiny to us, like little seeds, but then it bursts out, takes over, and fills the whole world! Help us get in on your kingdom life, and see it around us.

Plant: Luke 13:18-30

Water:

» Draw it: Make a drawing of your favorite image from today's story. (There are lots to choose from!)

» Plant it: During this season of Kingdomtide, we're talking about how God's kingdom grows in us and all around us. Get some easy-to-grow seeds, a small pot, and some soil, and let kids plant them today. (Wheatgrass is one easy option—it'll grow anywhere.) Notice how tiny the seeds are! Then, let the kids water it each day.

» Seek it: Look today for tiny little things that show you God's rule and power—a lovely plant, a kitten, a small act of kindness, a ladybug. Give praise to God for the tiny things that are good!

Weed: Where did you see God's kingdom in tiny things today? How did it make you feel to seek God's rule and power today? What are you grateful for today?

Thursday

Till: Gather us in Lord, under your wings. Hide us in your arms, so that we can be safe with you. We want to be near you today.

Plant: Luke 13:31-35

Water:

» Act it: Jesus tells us that God longs to gather us into his arms, so that we know we're safe. Demonstrate this for your kids: one by one, gather each in your arms, and tell them something you love about them. (You might have older kids do this for their younger siblings as well.)

» Apply it: What is one way you could live as if gathered in God's arms today? How could you remember that he is close?

» Water it: Make sure you water your kingdom plant today!

Weed: When did you remember to live "gathered close to God" today? When did you forget? When do you need to be close to God tomorrow? How can you remember him then?

Friday

Till: Jesus, you see right through our pretending. We act like we're big stuff, but you want us to know how to love everyone. Help us have humble, loving hearts.

Plant: Luke 14:1-11

Water:

» Imagine it: In today's story, Jesus cuts right to the heart of how we pretend in order to impress people. How would it feel to be the person who shoved their way to the important seat, only to be asked to go sit at the kids' table in the corner? How would it feel to choose to sit in the worst seat? How would it feel to be asked to come to the head of the table, the seat of honor?

» Apply it: When do you feel like you need to show that you're important and get the best for yourself? Today, how could you focus instead on helping someone else feel loved and honored?

» Water it: Make sure you water your kingdom plant today!

Weed: Today, did you push your way to the front at any point? When did you choose to show love and generosity instead of getting the best for yourself? How can you be generous tomorrow?

Saturday

Till: Jesus, you know our tricky hearts. Even as we act like we love, we're often just making sure we get paid back for our kindness. Help us to love people who have nothing we want.

Plant: Luke 14:12-24

Water:

» Draw it: Create a picture of a dinner table. Put a few dignified, rich people at the table, but then put in people who "don't belong" there—the poor, misfits, the dirty or smelly, or other people who get overlooked. How do you think the dignified people might feel? How do you think God would feel about this party?

» Apply it: Jesus knows our hearts: he knows that a lot of the time, we show love only to people who can love us back. He says that we should grow a heart that abounds in love even to those who can't repay us. Today, when could you show love to someone you don't think has anything to offer you in return?

» Water it: Make sure you water your kingdom plant today!

Weed: What was it like to offer love to someone who could not love you back? How did you feel? How did they feel? How do you think God felt? When could you do the same thing tomorrow? What are you grateful for today?

Week of Sunday closest to May 25

Sunday

Till: God, help us live in your kingdom, where we can have good, healthy hearts that produce good, healthy fruit. Help us not be impressed with fake, hollow fruit, but recognize your life all around us.

Plant: Matthew 12:33-45

Water:

» Apply it: Jesus teaches us that what's on the inside always shows up eventually on the outside. The hard evidence that God is in something is plain to see: if there's real, tangible love and joy and peace and kindness flowing out of someone, there God is! But the Pharisees didn't want to see it. Why do you think they couldn't see Jesus' fruit and believe?

» Seek it: Today be on the lookout—be on the hunt—for good fruit all around you. When you see love, or peace, or joy, or patience, or kindness, or self-control, praise Jesus! Do a happy dance!

» Water it: Make sure you water your kingdom plant today!

Weed: Where did you see good fruit today? How did it feel to praise Jesus for the good fruit? What are you most grateful for today?

Monday

Till: Jesus, help us to put down our grasping attempts to manage our own lives, and instead let us trust you today.

Plant: Luke 14:25-35

Water:

» Draw it: Make a drawing of either the builder who couldn't finish his castle, or the king who doesn't have enough troops at battle. Why do they look silly?

» Apply it: Following Jesus as his students means we trust him more than the things that we love—even more than our moms and dads, brothers and sisters—more than anything. Jesus tells us that even if we lost everything we love, we'd still be okay. Why do you think Jesus tells us that any cost will be worth it? How could it be okay to lose what you love? (Loss is a lifetime condition. Expressing the pain of loss within the context of a loving family is healing. Open the space to share without judgment.)

» Water it: Make sure you water your kingdom plant today!

Weed: What are some things you loved about today? Try to name a few ways God is better even than those things you enjoyed.

Tuesday

Till: Jesus, you go after the lost sheep, the lost coin—after the person who everyone thinks is lost and beyond help. Thank you for helping the helpless!

Plant: Luke 15:1-10

Water:

» Draw it: Think of a few people that we might sometimes consider beyond helping—maybe someone in prison, someone who is very poor, or someone who is really mean. Now, draw Jesus with them and angels partying as he rescues them!

» Imagine it: Picture the biggest bullies you can imagine. How do they treat other kids? How do you feel about them? Now, imagine: how do you think they would feel if they knew Jesus loves them so, so much? How do you think it would change them if they saw God and the angels celebrating with them as Jesus rescues them?

» Water it: Make sure you water your kingdom plant today!

Weed: Think over today or the past few days. Has there been anyone you didn't like, who you thought was not worth helping or loving? How could you show love to them tomorrow (or next time you see them), and show them that Jesus is seeking them? How did God show you he loved you today?

Wednesday

Till: God, you're a good father—you search after your children, welcoming them home! You forgive us when we run from you, and you forgive us when we demand things from you. Thank you for your forgiveness!

Plant: Luke 15:1-2, 11-32

Water:

» Act it: Play out this story! You'll need a father, a younger son, an older son, and maybe a friend, a pig, and a servant.

» Enter it: What does the father forgive the younger son for? How have you been like him? What does the father forgive the older son for? When have you been like him?

» Water it: Make sure you water your kingdom plant today!

Weed: Was there a time when you were like the younger brother today, running from God and disobeying? Was there a time when you were like the older brother today, demanding from God, or judging others? Tell about a time today when you enjoyed God's love and forgiveness?

Thursday

Till: Jesus, help us to be smart for what is right—to do good as often as we can. That is really, really living! Help us find real life!

Plant: Luke 16:1-9

Water:

» Understand it: Why does the manager go to his master's debtors and tell them to reduce their bill? Why does the master praise him?

» Apply it: What is one difficult situation today that you could use creativity to honor God or love someone else?

» Water it: Make sure you water your kingdom plant today!

Weed: Did you get to use your creative thinking in a tricky situation to love someone today? When did you miss the opportunity to be creatively loving? What can you do differently tomorrow?

Friday

Till: Jesus, teach us to be honest and trustworthy in small things, so we can grow and grow to be trustworthy in anything you ask us to do!

Plant: Luke 16:10-17

Water:

» Enter it: Can you think of some examples of when you have to learn to be trustworthy in a small thing, before you can move on to a big thing?

» Apply it: What small things can you be trustworthy in today? Ask God to help you do that.

» Water it: Make sure you water your kingdom plant today!

Weed: How were you trustworthy in small things today? Was there a time when you didn't act in an honest way? How could you do this different tomorrow with God?

Saturday

Till: Jesus, help us to have our eyes open to serve others around us while we can! Keep us from growing a heart that is cold to the needs of others, but instead help us search out opportunities to love.

Plant: Luke 16:19-31

Water:

» Apply it: God has shown us in the Bible that we should be about his business. His business is finding and serving people who need his love, wherever we are. Where could you share love or kindness today? Where could you keep your eyes open for people who need love or kindness?

» Water it: Make sure you water your kingdom plant today!

Weed: When did you see people who need love and kindness? How did you serve them? Did you forget, or close your eyes to anybody? Why? How could you do differently tomorrow?

Week of Sunday closest to June 1

Sunday

Till: Jesus, your kingdom has everything we need! It's the greatest find in the world! We want to live our lives in your care and your rule! May your kingdom grow!

Plant: Matthew 13:44-58

Water:

» Sculpt it: Jesus tells three little stories about what his kingdom is like. Use Silly Putty to make a sculpture that represents each one.

» Enter it: Why do you think God's kingdom is like a hidden treasure, or a priceless pearl, that we sell everything to get?

» Water it: Make sure you water your kingdom plant today!

Weed: Where did you see the kingdom of God today? Where can you look for the kingdom of God tomorrow? What are you most grateful for today?

Monday

Till: God, we don't want to do just the bare minimum and avoid trouble. We don't want to do just what we're told; we want to work with you! Help us learn to trust you and dream big for your kingdom.

Plant: Luke 17:1-10

Water:

» Play it: "Simon Says" is a game where you do only what you are told to do. Play the game with a twist: give instructions that require more than just that one action to complete. For example, "Simon Says draw me a picture" means that the child will have to get a piece of paper, pick up a crayon, etc. Do a few of these, and discuss what would happen if they couldn't do all those other actions.

» Imagine it: Can you imagine a situation where doing only what you are told to do, and no more, wouldn't be enough?

» Apply it: In today's reading, Jesus tells us that we shouldn't expect that if we do the bare minimum (which is just avoiding being bad) or just follow the rules that we will be good students of Jesus. Instead, we need to learn what is on God's heart and be creative with him. What is one thing God would be pleased by today, and how could you do it creatively?

» Water it: Make sure you water your kingdom plant today!

Weed: What was it like being creative to please God above-and-beyond today? Was there a time when you did the bare minimum, just to avoid trouble, instead of seeking to do good creatively? God believes all things good about you; how does that make you want to be creative?

Tuesday
....

Till: Thank you Jesus! Thank you for loving us! Thank you for healing us! Help us to say thank you all day long!

Plant: Luke 17:11-19

Water:

» Draw it: Draw out your favorite scene from this story.

» Enter it: God is so generous! He gives us everything we have and need. Make a list of blessings. See if you can write 10, then 20, good things in your life. You can start with Mom and Dad, and then go to the smell of flowers and to the taste of candy. Then, thank God for each one. Today, make a point to say "Thank you!" to God!

» Water it: Make sure you water your kingdom plant today!

Weed: What was it like saying "Thank you" to God? What did you forgot to say "Thank you" for? Thank God now.

Wednesday
....

Till: Let your kingdom come, Jesus! Help us to be ready to see your kingdom when it shows up!

Plant: Luke 17:20-37

Water:

» Enter it: When have you seen God show up unexpectedly? (Maybe He helped you, or you saw someone be kind or loving instead of selfish.)

» Apply it: Today, keep your eyes open for God.

» Water it: Make sure you water your kingdom plant today!

Weed: Where did you see God today? What distracted you from looking for God? How could you do differently tomorrow? What are you most grateful for today?

Thursday

Till: Lord, help us! We need you so much, so we're going to ask and ask and ask for your help. We'll keep asking because we know you love to help and you love to give. Lord, help us!

Plant: Luke 18:1-8

Water:

> » Enter it: Can you think of a time when you needed help, asked for it, and got it? What kind of help did you receive?

> » Apply it: We live with God by asking. We don't demand from God, but we can always ask. What might you ask God to help you with today?

> » Water it: Make sure you water your kingdom plant today!

Weed: When did you ask for God's help today? What happened? When did you need but didn't ask? Why do you think that is?

Friday

Till: God, give us mercy. Forgive us simple sinners, and help us live with you today. Thank you for your mercy!

Plant: Luke 18:9-14

Water:

» Enter it: In this story, the Pharisee puts on a pose and acts like he is great, but really he's just the same as the tax man, because he needs God's mercy just as much. Tell about a time when you have been tempted to think that you are better than someone else.

» Apply it: Try an experiment: throughout your day, repeat this prayer: "God, give me mercy. Forgive me, a sinner." Say it as often as you can, when you're walking and sitting and playing. You can say it silently. See what happens.

» Water it: Make sure you water your kingdom plant today!

Weed: What was it like to repeat this prayer? Did the prayer change your attitude toward other people? When did you see kindness today?

Saturday

Till: God, help us know when we trust in other things more than we trust in you. Help us to let those things go, and cling only to you instead! You are strong and steady and we can trust you!

Plant: Luke 18:15-30

Water:

» Draw it: Sketch out your favorite scene from this story.

» Enter it: Jesus asks the rich young ruler to let go of his money, not because money is bad, but because the man had started to trust his money more than God. In fact, money had become his God. So Jesus invited him to trust God alone. Can you think of some things you tend to trust in? Would it be better to trust God?

» Water it: Make sure you water your kingdom plant today!

Weed: When did you put your trust in God today? When did you put your trust in other things today? How did either of these make you feel?

Week of Sunday closest to June 8

....

Sunday
....

Till: Jesus, your love is so strong. You care for our daily needs, like loving through the gift of simple bread. Help us to show that same love to others.

Plant: Matthew 15:29-39

Water:

» Imagine it: How do you think it felt to be one of Jesus' disciples when he asked them to feed everyone? How do you think it felt to watch Jesus miraculously provide enough for everyone? How would you react?

» Live it: We may not be able to divide food miraculously right now, but we can join Jesus in caring about those who are hungry. As a family find a time that you can serve in a food bank, homeless shelter, or soup kitchen.

» Water it: Make sure you water your kingdom plant today!

Weed: When did you see someone who was in need? Did you help? How could you keep an eye out for need tomorrow? When did you see generosity today?

Monday
·········

Till: Jesus! Son of David! Mercy! Have mercy on us! We want to be made whole. We want to see you. Have mercy on us!

Plant: Luke 18:31-43

Water:

> » Define it: How would you define mercy? What does mercy look like?

> » Apply it: Where do you think you need God's mercy today? How could you ask for it? How can you show mercy to others?

> » Water it: Make sure you water your kingdom plant today!

Weed: When did you ask for mercy today? When do you think you will need mercy tomorrow? What does it mean to be filled with mercy? What would that look like?

Tuesday
·········

Till: Jesus, you came to search out the spiritual zeroes, the people who were wandering far away from God. We ask for your salvation. We need you to set us free from everything that keeps us from you!

Plant: Luke 19:1-10

Water:

> » Define it: What do you think "salvation" means? What would it look like to be "saved" from prison? To be "saved" from a bad habit? To be "saved" from an argument with a friend?

> » Enter it: Where are some places you think you need salvation? What might it look like to get it?

» Ask it: Write or say a prayer today asking for Jesus to come and bring salvation to your whole life. Be specific. What would you like Jesus to set you free from?

Weed: What was it like asking for salvation? Are there areas you don't like to ask for help with? Why not?

Wednesday

Till: Jesus, you are so good! You invite us to be a part of what you're doing in the world! We get to share in what makes you happy! Help us to be responsible and creative with whatever you give us to do.

Plant: Luke 19:11-27

Water:

» Understand it: Why do you think the two servants were eager to double their master's money? Why do you think the last servant was afraid and hid the money?

» Enter it: What are some abilities, talents, and gifts that God has given you? How could those be used for his kingdom?

» Apply it: Choose one way today that you can use your gifts and talents to grow God's kingdom.

» Water it: Make sure you water your kingdom plant today!

Weed: How did you use your talents for God's kingdom today? How does it feel to know that you get to play a part in God's plan for good? What are you most grateful for today?

Thursday

Till: Hosanna! Hosanna! Blessed are you Jesus, you come in God's name as our king! Hosanna!

Plant: Luke 19:28-40

Water:

» Draw it: Make a drawing of Jesus entering the city while everyone praises him.

» Welcome it: Jesus is our King! Where can you welcome his rule today?

» Water it: Make sure you water your kingdom plant today!

Weed: When did you welcome God's rule today? Was there a time when you didn't want to welcome Jesus' rule, but instead wanted to do your own thing? Tell God about that, then pause and imagine his love washing over you. He loves you no matter what.

Friday

Till: Oh Jesus, things aren't right in the world. There is violence and war, lying and stealing, hate and sadness. We need your help so much! Please come, Jesus.

Plant: Luke 19:41-48

Water:

» Mourning it: It's easy to close our eyes to suffering in the world, but Jesus kept his eyes open and wept over it. There is so much that isn't right! As a family, look over a newspaper and pray for those who are in trouble or hurting. Weep with those who are having a hard time.

» Welcome it: Just like we did yesterday, we can look forward to and welcome Jesus' rule. Today, welcome Jesus' rule whenever you see or hear something sad. Ask for him to come.

» Water it: Make sure you water your kingdom plant today!

Weed: When did you welcome Jesus today? What was sad today? Tell God about these things, then pause and imagine his love washing over you.

Saturday

Till: Jesus, you are the Word. Help us to use words the way you do. Help us use words to tell the truth, communicate love, encourage and give life. Teach us to use our words well.

Plant: Luke 20:1-8

Water:

» Draw it: Draw the huddle of Pharisees trying to find a way out of Jesus' question. Why do you think they don't want to answer him?

» Enter it: The Pharisees are trying to use their words in a tricky way to get out of the truth. When do you tend to use words in a tricky way?

» Apply it: Today, try to use your words only to speak the truth and love people. See what happens.

» Water it: Make sure you water your kingdom plant today!

Weed: When did you use words to speak the truth? When did you use words in a tricky way? Why do you think you did that? Tell God about these things, then pause and imagine his love washing over you.

Week of Sunday closest to June 15

Sunday

Till: Jesus, help us to stay simple and trusting. You are everything we need, and you provide for us. We can trust you, so we don't need to become proud or seize control. Today, we'll trust and rest in you.

Plant: Matthew 18:1-14

Water:

» List it: Make a list of reasons you can trust God. See how long you can make your list.

» Live it: What is one way you could trust God today instead of worrying?

» Water it: Make sure you water your kingdom plant today!

Weed: Did you worry today? When did you trust God today? Tell God about your worries, then pause and imagine his love washing over you.

Monday
. . . .

Till: Jesus, help us be faithful servants in your vineyard! Teach us to use our energy to work alongside you.

Plant: Luke 20:9-19

Water:

» Draw it: Instead of drawing the unfaithful workers, draw a picture of you working with God in his vineyard. How do you feel to be working with God? How does God feel to have you working with him?

» Apply it: How can you work with God today?

» Water it: Make sure you water your kingdom plant today!

Weed: When did you work with God today? What was it like to work with God? What are you most grateful for today? What are you least grateful for today?

Tuesday
. . . .

Till: Jesus, we praise you because you know everything! You are the smartest person who ever lived. You see right through our hearts, and you know what's best for us.

Plant: Luke 20:19-26

Water:

» List it: Jesus is smart! He saw right through the plot of the Pharisees, and his answer was so brilliant that they were speechless. Make a list: What are some things that Jesus knows? What are some things he understands? See how long you can make your list.

» Celebrate it: Today, have a celebration of Jesus' mind! Have everyone in the family dress up like doctors, professors, or all-around smart people. Name aloud some things from your list, and praise Jesus! Play some smart music (such as Bach or Mozart) and dance!

» Water it: Make sure you water your kingdom plant today!

Weed: How does it feel to know that Jesus is the smartest person ever? What are you most grateful for today? What are you least grateful for today?

Wednesday
. . . .

Till: You are God of the living! God, those who are your friends will live with you forever and ever. Thank you for promising us eternal life!

Plant: Luke 20:27-40

Water:

» Draw it: Jesus lets us know beyond a doubt that those who are friends of God—people like Abraham, Isaac, and Jacob—don't stay dead, but live with God forever. Make a picture of God sitting down to a meal with some of his friends. Include your favorite Bible heroes (Ruth, David, Peter, Paul, etc). Be sure to draw yourself and your family there with Him also!

» Apply it: How does it make you feel to know that God has a forever-and-ever plan to keep you close to him? How could you remember that throughout this day?

» Water it: Make sure you water your kingdom plant today!

Weed: How did it make a difference today knowing that God will keep you alive with him forever? How might it make a difference tomorrow?

Thursday

Till: God, you don't look at our bank accounts, you look at our hearts. You are pleased when we love to give and help others. Teach us to love like you do!

Plant: Luke 20:41-21:4

Water:

» Give it: In today's story, Jesus compares the "religious" people who like to show off with a poor widow who gave only two pennies that she really couldn't afford to give! The widow gave more because she was the one who was really trusting God. Try an experiment: can you think of something that you don't think you can give up, and offer it to someone in need? (Note to parents: Don't force this activity. Giving has to come from the heart. You might talk about what it's like to live without the basic things you need, to help your kids understand. But if they are unwilling, it won't help for you to force them or guilt-trip them. Instead set the example through your own life.)

» Water it: Make sure you water your kingdom plant today!

Weed: What was it like giving something up today? How do you think God felt about what you offered? What were you most grateful for today? What were you least grateful for today?

Friday

Till: God, help us to stay with you, trusting in you, to the very end. Even if things fall apart, you are faithful. Help us have endurance.

Plant: Luke 21:5-19

Water:

» Imagine it: Jesus tells us that some scary things can happen, but they don't mean God is far away. He says every detail of our body and soul—even every single hair!—matters to God. Imagine what it would be like for God to be paying attention to every single hair on your head. How do you feel imagining that God is always watching every single part of you in order to help you?

»   Apply it: How could you remind yourself today that God is watching over you?

»   Water it: Make sure you water your kingdom plant today!

Weed: When did you remember that God is keeping watch over you? Did you forget at any point?

Saturday

Till: God, when things look like they couldn't get any worse, you're not far away! Help us to trust you in our trouble.

Plant: Luke 21:20-28

Water:

»   Remember it: Tell about a time when things seemed like they couldn't get any worse? How did God help you?

»   Live it: Today, when things go wrong or don't go your way, how could you be reminded that God isn't far off and will help?

»   Water it: Make sure you water your kingdom plant today! (Since it's been six weeks, we figure that you're either in the rhythm of watering your plant, or it's long gone by now. We won't remind you every day any more, but if it's alive, keep it up!)

Weed: Where was there trouble today? Did you remember God? Tell God about the trouble you experienced, then pause and imagine that his love is washing over you.

Week of Sunday closest to June 22

Sunday

Till: Jesus, we may have to lose other things as we follow you, but we get you! We get life with God, forever and ever! So we get everything!

Plant: Matthew 19:23-30

Water:

> » Release it: Make a list of all the things you really love. Next to each, write one way that God is better. For example, "Chocolate: Once I eat it, it's gone. However God is never gone!"

> » Live it: Pick one of the things off your list. How can you use and live with this today in a way that shows that God is more satisfying?

Weed: When was God satisfying today? What are you most grateful for today? What are you least grateful for today?

Monday

Till: God, help us to remember you. There are so many distractions. Entertaining television, fascinating books, fun games, and enjoyable friends can all be distractions. Help us receive these things as gifts from you, but keep you at the center of our hearts.

Plant: Luke 21:29-36

Water:

» Think it: When you're starving for dinner, what happens if you eat a bunch of cookies and snacks? What do you think happens to your love for God if you continually keep yourself entertained and getting everything you want?

» Wait for him: Today, spend some time in quietly waiting on God. Find a space where you can be alone and quiet. Don't take a book, or computer games, or toys. Just spend ten minutes quiet, making room for your heart to want God. See what happens.

Weed: How did it feel to wait for God? Tell about a time today when you were patient. Tell God about these things, then pause and imagine God's love pouring all over you.

Tuesday

Till: Jesus, you know the pain of betrayal. Help us to trust in you when people treat us badly, especially when it's our friends who hurt us.

Plant: Luke 21:37-22:13

Water:

» Remember it: In this story, one of Jesus' closest disciples agrees to betray him, for money! Share a time when a close friend hurt you badly. How did it feel?

» Live it: How does it make you feel to know that Jesus understands that pain? What might you share with him the next time someone hurts you?

Weed: Did anyone hurt your feelings today? Tell Jesus about that. Do you think you hurt anyone's feelings today, intentionally or not? Tell Jesus about that too, then pause and imagine God's love pouring all over you.

Wednesday

Till: We remember you, Jesus! Your body was broken and your blood spilled, we know God loves us. Thank you for giving your life for us.

Plant: Luke 22:14-23

Water:

» Celebrate it: Today, share Communion as a family. Reread today's passage, then share the bread and cup together. (If you are part of a church tradition where only priests may offer communion, then talk about what the elements mean.)

Weed: When today did you remember that Jesus died for you? Tell Jesus about that, then pause and imagine God's love pouring all over you.

Thursday

Till: Jesus, even though you are King, you came among us as a servant! Help us to learn from you how to serve others today.

Plant: Luke 22:24-30

Water:

» Live it: Jesus is teaching us that, in his kingdom, the greatest sign of power and strength is to care for other people and serve them. God's royal authority enables us, not so that we can boss others around, but to help them when they are in need. Who can you serve today? Try helping as much as you can today.

Weed: Who did you help today? When were you like Jesus in serving others? Did you boss anyone around or try to be powerful by being served? Tell Jesus about these things, then pause and imagine God's love pouring all over you.

Friday
· · · · · ·

Till: Jesus, you know that we are weak and feeble. Thank you for praying for us today. Thank you for asking God to give us strength and keep us humble.

Plant: Luke 22:31-38

Water:

» Draw it: Think of a time when you feel weak or tempted. Create a picture of yourself in that situation, and draw Jesus right there, praying for you.

» Apply it: What does it mean for you today that Jesus prays for you in your weakness?

Weed: When did you feel weak today? How did you remember that Jesus was praying for you? Tell these things to Jesus, then pause and imagine God's love pouring all over you.

Saturday

. . . .

Till: Oh Lord, there are things we want you to give us, and things we want you to take away. But don't do what we want; do what you want. Your way is best for us, Lord. Teach us to want your way more than our own way.

Plant: Luke 22:39-51

Water:

» Imagine it: In today's story, Jesus is distressed, and he asks his father to take away the thing he is worried about. But then he says, "Not my will, but yours be done." How can Jesus say this?

» Live it: Today, use this prayer in hard situations: "Not what I want; what you want." See what happens.

Weed: When did you pray, "Not what I want, but what you want" today? How did that feel? What gave you joy or sorrow today?

Week of Sunday closest to June 29

Sunday

Till: Help us, Lord Jesus, to see that our good deeds must come from our hearts. Create in us a clean heart, a clean inside.

Plant: Matthew 21:23-32

Water:

» Wash it: Tonight after dinner, wash the dishes with the children, but only wash the outsides of the dishes. See who notices first. Discuss what Jesus meant by cleaning the outside and not the inside.

» Tell it: Tell about a time when someone has said they were sorry to you, but they didn't mean it. How did it feel? What do you think that has to do with what Jesus says about good actions coming from our hearts?

Weed: What good did you do today? Did that good come from your heart, or did you want others to think you were good?

Monday

Till: Lord Jesus, help us to walk closely with you. Help us to tell others about you by the way we act. We want to be kind and compassionate, but we need your help.

Plant: Luke 22:52-62

Water:

» Act it: Assign parts and act out the scene. Discuss what might have happened if Peter would have said, "Yes, I know him. He is my Lord and friend."

» Discuss it: How do our actions tell others that we know Jesus?

Weed: Were there ways that you denied Jesus by your actions today? Were there ways that you said, "Yes, I know him. He is my Lord and friend." by your actions today? Tell Jesus about this, then pause and imagine the love of God pouring out all over you.

Tuesday

Till: Jesus, it makes us sad that you were abused. Those people were hitting you and you didn't hit back. They were making fun of you and calling you names, but you didn't give them what they deserved. You loved them instead. Help us to remember when people treat us badly that we are not alone.

Plant: Luke 22:63-71

Water:

» Discuss it: Tell about a time when you have been hurt. (Parent, please share carefully about a time when you have been hurt. It is important for children, all people, to know that they don't suffer alone.)

» Pray it: Pray with those who shared. Ask for God's intervention, his comfort, his protection. (As you are listening pray for discernment. Is your child, or are you, struggling with forgiveness and anger, or is there need for comfort and protection?)

Weed: Did you see someone being hurt today? What did you do? How did you feel? Were you hurt today? Tell Jesus about these hurts, then pause and imagine the tender, love of God pouring out all over you.

Wednesday

Till: Lord Jesus, our hearts are saddened by the way you were treated. Help us to follow you, instead of trying to get you to follow us.

Plant: Luke 23:1-12

Water:

> » Play it: Play "Follow the Leader." Give each member a chance to be the teacher. Then read Matthew 4:18-20. Talk about how we follow Jesus. Herod wanted Jesus to follow him, but Jesus knew better.

> » Discuss it: It is Jesus who calls us to follow him. Tell about a time when you wanted Jesus to follow you? How can you follow Jesus today?

Weed: How did you follow Jesus today? When did you catch yourself asking Jesus to follow you? What is drawing you to God or away from God?

Thursday

Till: Lord Jesus, help us to listen to your still, small, voice instead of the shouting crowd. Teach us to really listen.

Plant: Luke 23:13-25

Water:

» Enter it: Ask the children to look into their hearts and identify who they were in the scene. Were they:

  » Pilate, the one who tried to hear from God but was shouted down;

  » The crowd, the people who followed Jesus early on, but turned against him;

  » High priests and rulers, those who are always accusing others, but never looking at themselves;

  » Barabbas, one who is guilty, but is set free;

  » Or even Jesus, one who is accused wrongly and will suffer for others.

» Journal it: Invite children to write or draw who they are and why, then listen quietly to what the Holy Spirit wants to say to them throughout the day.

Weed: Share with the family who you were in today's story? After each family member shares, everyone join together and pray for that person.

Friday
......

Till: Jesus you called us to follow you, and if we follow you we have to give up getting our way. We have to follow you like Simon from Cyrene carrying the cross. Help us Jesus we can't do it alone.

Plant: Luke 23:26-31

Water:

» List it: Very early in Jesus' ministry he asked people to follow him. That means we follow him when life is easy and when, like Simon of Cyrene,

Jesus goes to the cross. As a family make a list of easy times to follow Jesus and hard times to follow Jesus.

» Discuss it: Discuss the hard times, and the ways you can help each other. Read Corrie ten Boom's book, *The Hiding Place*, together over the next few weeks. Discuss how she and her family followed Jesus when it was hard.

Weed: Tell about a time today it was easy to follow Jesus. Tell about a time today when it was hard to follow Jesus.

Saturday

Till: Lord Jesus, help us! Help us to bless instead of curse. Help us to love instead of poke fun. Forgive us when we fail.

Plant: Luke 23:32-43

Water:

» Imagine it: Invite everyone (except the reader) to close their eyes and imagine they are in the story. Reread the passage two times, pausing briefly in between each reading. Invite the Holy Spirit to speak to your hearts.

» Share it: What did the Holy Spirit speak to you about? Who were you in the story? What questions does this passage bring to your mind?

Weed: As you went through your day, when did you think of today's scripture? What were your thoughts? Did you see people today who were "cursing" others? Did you see people today who were blessing others? What kind of person were you today?

Week of Sunday closest to July 6

Sunday

Till: Lord, you love parties! Your kingdom is a wonderful life party that you have invited everyone to. Help us to follow you into it.

Plant: Matthew 22:1-14

Water:

» Act it: Invite family members to act out the scene. Have one reader and everyone else as actors.

» Discuss it: Ask, "Whose fault is it that some didn't go to the party? Who did the King invite? In what ways can you accept God's invitation to "his party," or living in the kingdom of God?" (For example: When we live in God's kingdom, we don't worry because we know he is in charge and he loves us and will work things out for our good. We are willing to be last, we don't have to have our way, and we stick up for others who are treated badly. We are honest and kind, and show compassion. This is how we know we are living in God's kingdom.)

Weed: How did you accept God's invitation and live in his kingdom today? In what ways did you reject God's invitation and not live in his kingdom? Invite family members to pray for each other to live more fully in God's kingdom.

Monday

Till: Oh Lord Jesus, we mourn your death. But here in the middle of such sadness is Joseph of Arimathea. He was looking for your kingdom. He knew that you could help us live in it. Help us to learn from him.

Plant: Luke 23:44-56

Water:

» Be alert: Play "Duck, Duck, Goose"! Invite everyone to play no matter their age. Then discuss how it felt to be alert and ready to be tagged.

» Discuss it: Joseph of Arimathea "lived in alert expectation of the kingdom of God." Thinking back to yesterday's story, which of the guests lived in alert expectation? How can you live that way today?

Weed: Tell about a time today when you lived in alert expectation of the kingdom of God. When today were you aware that God was with you?

Tuesday

Till: We are so amazed and filled with joy that we might burst. You beat death, so we will never die. This is great news!

Plant: Luke 23:56-24:11

Water:

» Act it: This is the most jubilant scene in the entire Bible. Act it out with all the excitement of dynamite.

» Discuss it: It really is the best news that Jesus beat death. Talk as a family about bodies and spirits. Discuss how bodies die, but spirits live forever. (*Renovation of the Heart* by Dallas Willard is a superb book about the parts of the person.)

Weed: Since you are going to live forever, what did you do today that will last forever? Keeping in mind that people last forever, not things; what can you do tomorrow that will last forever?

Wednesday

Till: Lord God, you made us and you know exactly how to show yourself to us so that we can understand. Thank you for doing ordinary things like walking with us, and eat supper with us. Help us to look for you in the ordinary things we do each day.

Plant: Luke 24:13-35

Water:

>> Cook it: Choose a meal today that you can make as a family. Everybody helps. Everybody eats.

>> Look for it: What are some ordinary things you will do today? How can you look for Jesus?

Weed: Where did you see Jesus in the ordinary today? What was your response to seeing him? When did you feel the most free or the least free?

Thursday

Till: Jesus, often we don't understand the Bible. Like the disciples we think we know, but we don't. Teach us; help us to understand with our hearts and our minds so we too can burst with joy.

Plant: Luke 24:36-53

Water:

> » Act it: This is such a great scene! Invite family members to act it out while someone else reads it.

> » Discuss it: Often human beings misunderstand the Bible and do great harm. Jesus took the Old Testament (remember there was no New Testament at this time) and showed his disciples how he was already in it. Each story in the Old Testament whispers the name of Jesus. As we read the stories and look for him, we will find him and our understanding will be clearer.

Weed: Take time this evening and read one of the Minor Prophets in the Old Testament (their books are Hosea through Malachi). See if you can hear the book whisper the name of Jesus? Today you can also begin reading Exodus, asking how God helps Moses to become more like Jesus.

Friday
......

Till: God, bless us with understanding as we read the Bible today. Holy Spirit, use it to change us from the inside out.

Plant: Mark 1:1-13

Water:

> » Remember it: Tell your family stories about who was or is the messiest eater when he or she was a baby? My (Lacy's) brother was a food thrower, and my eldest daughter was a forehead food smasher. Talk about how food that didn't get into the mouth and swallowed was useless. It might have been entertaining, but it didn't help feed the baby.

> » Discuss it: John the Baptist tells us that our hearts are fed in a similar way. We can't make ourselves be good to others when we don't want to, unless Jesus has already fed our hearts. When we spend time with Jesus—through prayer, Bible reading, listening, serving others—he

feeds our hearts and they change to become more like his, and then being good is easy.

Weed: In what ways did you spend time with Jesus so he could feed your heart? When did you just "throw food," and not really eat anything, just trying to be good?

Saturday

Till: Jesus, help us to really know who you are. With one call, Simon, Andrew, James, and John dropped everything and followed you. Even demonic spirits obey you immediately. You are the Holy Son of God. Blessed be your name.

Plant: Mark 1:14-28

Water:

> » Create it: Make a praise banner. Use the side of a large cardboard box, butcher paper, or poster board. Brainstorm a list of all the wonderful attributes of Jesus. Design it as a family, but let the littlest people decorate it.

> » Worship him: Sing praise songs or play a praise CD everyone can sing along to.

Weed: When did you think about Jesus today? Share about a time today when your mind thought back to the worship songs from this morning.

Week of Sunday closest to July 13

Sunday

Till: Help us, Jesus, to open our hearts to your good news. You did come to bring us good news; help us to look for you and welcome you with our hearts open.

Plant: Matthew 23:29-39

Water:

» Open it: Blindfold one member of the family. Now spin them a time or two and then have them try to find and enter their bedroom. (Close their bedroom door before starting.) Talk about the differences in finding and entering the bedroom with eyes open, door open verses eyes blinded, door shut.

» Discuss it: In order to hear Jesus we must make time to actually listen quietly to him. In order to know where we are going we have to look for Jesus in all we do. How can we listen and look today?

Weed: When did you take the time to be quiet and listen to the voice of Jesus? Where did you see Jesus today? What gave you joy or sorrow today?

Monday
. . . .

Till: Oh Jesus, you know us. You know that when our lives have been touched by you, we can't keep quiet. We tell everyone!

Plant: Mark 1:29-45

Water:

» Tell it: When Jesus touches our lives we can't seem to keep from telling everyone. Take time this morning to tell your story about a time Jesus has touched your life.

» Worship him: It is natural for worship to follow telling our stories. This morning sing a praise song together, or sing along with a praise CD.

Weed: What did it feel like to tell your story? Did you tell it again to anyone else? At what point in your day did the words of one of the praise songs come back into your mind?

Tuesday
. . . .

Till: Jesus, we can't believe our ears! All the miracles that you did and are still doing today amaze us. Thank you for living with us! It IS great news.

Plant: Mark 2:1-12

Water:

» Puppet it: Invite the younger members to make a puppet show out of today's scene. Use old socks as puppets and a large cardboard box. (Appliance stores have lots of them.)

» Give thanks: Thankfulness leads to worship. Begin a thankful prayer— all family members can pray a simple prayer, "Thank you God for…"— and continue saying all that comes to your mind. Feel free to speak over one another, letting the sweet smell of your family's praise and thankfulness spill into the heavens.

Weed: Enjoy the puppet show! Start a family thankfulness journal. This summer write in it nightly. Be sure to date the entries.

Wednesday

Till: Jesus, thank you for bringing the good news of God's kingdom. Help us to understand what it means and to celebrate.

Plant: Mark 2:13-22

Water:

» List it: Give each person a sheet of paper and a pencil; if they have journals they can use them. Draw a line down the middle of the page. At the top of one side write "Kingdom of God" and on the other side write "Kingdom of Me." Make a list of what life is like in each kingdom. (Example: Under "Kingdom of God", I am perfectly safe because God loves me and will do what is best, keeping nothing but giving everything, loving others, loving myself. Under "Kingdom of Me", I am not safe; serving myself first means never really loving others and that leads to being all by myself; choosing my way over God's way leads to many trips and falls.)

» Celebrate it: Plan a kingdom of God party. Using your lists make a banner celebrating that the kingdom of God is here! Have special desserts, play games, rent a karaoke machine, have fun!

Weed: When did you live in the Kingdom of God today? When did you live in the Kingdom of Me today? When did you feel the most or least free today?

Thursday

Till: You are Lord of the Sabbath and we are not. In your wisdom you taught us to rest. In ours we often do not. Help us to learn from you, for your burdens are easy and light.

Plant: Mark 2:23-3:6

Water:

» Sabbath it: In our home (Lacy's) we can't always Sabbath on Sunday or even Saturday, but we try to choose one day a week where as a family we rest. Often doing good for someone else is as life-giving as napping. What can your family do to honor the Sabbath weekly?

» Plan it: Discuss what you might like to do or not do to honor the Sabbath this week. The only rule is that you honor the Sabbath together, because the Sabbath is a community commandment.

Weed: Our days are often filled with little Sabbaths, small swatches of time that are life giving and full of rest. Did your day involve any little Sabbaths? If so, when? If not, how can you make a place for them?

Friday

Till: Jesus, you gave yourself to all of us. Some only want to be healed, some only want to get a look at you, but some of us want to really know you like a friend, like we know our family.

Plant: Mark 3:7-19a

Water:

» Friend it: Discuss how people make friends and keep them. Our families are the people who know us the best because we spend lots of time together. We talk and listen to each other. How is getting to know Jesus like getting to know friends or the members of our family? (Example:

"I've often wondered why Jesus was always telling demons and people not to identify him as the Son of God. Then it occurred to me that deep friendships don't happen with crowds of people, so Jesus chose twelve close friends out of the crowds.") Who are your close friends? How can you deepen your relationship with those people?

Weed: Say a prayer of thankfulness for the friends you have been given. How were you a good friend today? How were you not a good friend?

Saturday

Till: Thank you, Jesus, for welcoming us into your family! As we obey God and follow you we are included in a great big family.

Plant: Mark 3:20-35

Water:

» Big family: Make a list of family members and special friends who are like family, adding missionaries or pastors you know. This is your Big Family. Take a paper plate and trace on it the largest hands in the immediate family. Decorate the plate around the hands. On separates piece of paper draw a simple man (like a gingerbread man) or woman for each person on your list. Decorate the people. Place the people in the hands and leave the plate on the kitchen table. Each day each person should choose another person to pray for.

» Listen to it: Invite one member to read the passage while everyone closes their eyes and listens. Before beginning, pray a simple prayer asking the Holy Spirit to speak to you. Read the passage twice, pausing in between. Invite family to share how the Holy Spirit spoke to them.

Weed: Who did you see today that is in your Big Family? How did it feel knowing you were praying for them? How did it feel knowing others were praying for you?

Week of Sunday closest to July 20

Sunday

Till: Jesus, we forget that God is safe and loving. We are so afraid of disappointing you. Help us to live with confidence in our Father in heaven.

Plant: Matthew 25:14-30

Water:

» Act it: Assign parts, inviting the more verbal family members to add dialog. Assign the youngest child as the master and act it out. After the skit, ask "What is Jesus trying to tell his disciples?"

» List it: Brainstorm a list out loud of all the ways we can put our confidence in God. (Example: "When we are working with Him, we can do our very best, because nothing goes to waste with God. When making friends we don't have to pretend, we can be who we really are, because we are confident that God has made us rightly.")

Weed: In what ways did you act with confidence in God today? In what ways did you act as if God would not take care of you?

Monday

Till: Lord Jesus, open our eyes and our ears help us to understand the kingdom of God. Help us to want to live in it every day.

Plant: Mark 4:1-20

Water:

» Sculpt it: Use Silly Putty and invite individuals to each sculpt one of four scenes, from verses 14-15, 16-17, 18-19, and verse 20. As everyone is working talk about what the Jesus tells us the parable means.

» Reflect on it: After reading the scripture invite the family to journal or mentally reflect on the passage. We are all in difference scenes at different times; which scene are you in right now?

Weed: Did you see any of these scenes play out in your day? If so, tell about it. What gave you joy or sorrow today?

Tuesday

Till: Jesus, you are always reminding us, because we are forgetful, that the kingdom of God is NOT like the kingdom of this world. In God's kingdom there are no secrets, and we give instead of get. Help us to remember.

Plant: Mark 4:21-34

Water:

» Draw it: Cut a piece of poster board in half. On one side draw the scene from verses 26-29. On the other half draw the scene from verses 30-32. Write "The kingdom of God is here," in large letters on each half. Display in a space where everyone can be reminded before they leave for their day. (Maybe on the garage wall or near the front door, so it's the last thing you see.)

» Imagine it: There is nothing special about these stories except that they are ordinary. Jesus used ordinary everyday stuff to teach about the kingdom of God. Now it's your turn. Create a story, using the ordinary everyday stuff of your lives to teach about the kingdom of God.

Weed: What did you see today that reminded you of the kingdom of God? What did you do today that was living in the kingdom of God?

Wednesday

Till: Help us to remember that when we are with you, we are perfectly safe. Thank you for protecting us.

Plant: Mark 4:35-41

Water:

» Share it: Invite family members to share about a time when they thought that they were going to die. Paul reminds us that for Christians there is no bad news. If we live we live with Jesus and our family; if we die we still live with Jesus and soon enough our family as well.

» Discuss it: Ask, "When we're afraid what should we do?" Brainstorm some solutions with your family. (Examples: Pray, tell a family member and ask them to stay with you and pray with you, write a prayer to God about your fears.)

Weed: Was there a time today when it was hard to believe that you are perfectly safe? Tell Jesus about this, then imagine the protecting love of God flowing all over you.

Thursday

Till: Jesus, you remind us that often the best good we can do is right where we are. You have put us in this family, in this town, in this church and we are thankful. Help us, Lord Jesus, to know how you want to use us right where we are.

Plant: Mark 5:1-20

Water:

- » Act it: This story has so much action, as if especially tailored for a teen-aged boy. Invite someone to read it, while everyone else picks a part and acts it out.

- » Live it: The man who was healed from the demons wanted to physically follow Jesus. He knew being with Jesus was the best place to be. But Jesus had other work for the man. Jesus invited the man to partner with him. He was to go back to his home town and tell his story, become a preacher and lead others to Jesus. God wants to use us right where we are. Where are you? (Examples: School, home, work, church, community, doing sports or hobbies) How does God want to use you in all those places where you are?

Weed: What was life like for you today? When did you feel the most free or the least free?

Friday

Till: Lord, we are always asking, "Can we trust you?" We wonder if you will take care of us when bad things happen. We wonder if you will be kind when we come to you. Thank you for always answering, "Yes, yes, yes."

Plant: Mark 5:21-43

Water:

» Imagine it: Imagine that you are Jairus. Can you believe Jesus and not those who are saying that your daughter is dead? Discuss why or why not.

» Tune it out: Grab a radio, or use the radio in your car. Show the children that when the buttons are set on the right station we can hear it clearly, but change the buttons just a bit and you can barely hear it; change it a little more and you can't hear it at all. Tell them how people tune out too. We can change our focus or our buttons to be more on Jesus, and we can hear the rest of the world. Sometimes we need to do that. When we hear people telling what we know are lies, we can tune them out. When we hear people telling gossip about someone, we can tune them out. Discuss some other times it is good to tune others out.

Weed: When did you tune in to Jesus today? What were you most or least grateful for today?

Saturday

Till: We can barely believe that you, God, want to work with us. You don't want robots; you want people who will work with you. We are your people and we are excited.

Plant: Mark 6:1-13

Water:

» Notice it: Jesus gave his disciples instructions; read them again starting with verses 7-11. Did you notice they aren't specific instructions? He doesn't tell them how to deal with every little thing. He gives them guidelines. He trusts them, and even more than that he trusts that God has it all under control.

» Listen to it: Quietly read over the instructions again and ask the Holy Spirit to tell you what your instructions are for today. The leading of the Holy Spirit is often not a voice, but a leading or a nudging in a direction. Be still and listen.

Weed: What were your instructions for today? Did you follow them? Why or why not? When did you give or receive love today?

Week of Sunday closest to July 27

Sunday

Till: Lord Jesus, help us. Help us to see you in those that are overlooked by everyone else. Help us to remember those that the world forgets.

Plant: Matthew 25:31-46

Water:

» Work it: This is a powerful passage. Read it aloud again, inviting the Holy Spirit to speak to your hearts. Invite family members to share what they heard.

» Serve it: Is there a place in the community where your family can make a difference? Perhaps a weekly or monthly service at a soup kitchen, or maybe holding hands and listening to stories at the nursing home? Maybe teaching English to immigrant workers, or babysitting their children for free? Any of these serves the least of these in our community. This is how we learn to serve Jesus. If none of these strike your fancy, think of your town and ask. "Who are the overlooked? How can we serve them?"

Weed: When you were at work or school today, did you notice who was overlooked? When did you give or receive love today?

Monday

Till: Oh God, our home is with you and we know it. We long to be with you, and yet so often we choose our own way. Help us choose you.

Plant: Mark 6:14-29

Water:

» Puzzle it: If you have younger children enjoy a simple puzzle together. While you are working talk about how God is the missing piece in everyone's heart. Herod was in awe of John because John spoke for God. Herod knew he was missing a piece, but he loved himself more than he wanted to be whole. Many times when people behave badly it is for the same reason that Herod did: they know that God can fill the missing piece in their hearts and make them whole, but they won't let him do it.

» Discuss it: With older children talk about telling the truth when it's hard, or even scary. John told the truth about Herod and his adulterous relationship with his brother's wife, and it got him killed. Could you do it? Could you tell the truth even if it meant your life? Tell about a time it was difficult to tell the truth. John was able to tell the truth because he lived in the kingdom of God, where it is perfectly safe. Yes, Herod killed John's body, but his spirit never left the presence of God. John lost nothing but gained everything.

Weed: Did you see anyone behaving badly today? Did you think about how they are missing a piece in their heart? Pray for them now. Tell about a time today when it was difficult to tell the truth.

Tuesday

Till: We are amazed that the God of the universe wants to work with us. You created us in your image so that we could work with you in doing good. Help us see the chance to work with you and take it.

Plant: Mark 6:30-46

Water:

» Picture it: Take out a family photo album and look through it. Decide who looks like whom. (Did Mom get Aunt Karla's nose?) All humans also look like their Father in heaven. He made us in his image. That means that he gave us something he also has: the freedom to choose. We can choose to do good or bad. We can choose to love God or hate him. When he made us he wanted us to choose to work with him to spread goodness everywhere we go. What kind of good can you spread today?

» Partner it: God does have a plan to change the world, and he wants humans to execute it. Find a place by yourself and reread this passage of the Bible, making notes in your journal if you like. Listen for the Holy Spirit to speak to you. Ask him to show you how to work with him today.

Weed: How did you work with God today? What kind of good did you spread today? When did you feel the most or least free?

Wednesday

Till: Jesus, we know that you can heal anybody. We know that you love people very much. Help us to bring the sick people we know to you.

Plant: Mark 6:47-56

Water:

» Bring it: With older children read through the newspaper while listening for the Holy Spirit. When the Holy Spirit calls your attention to something, pray about it on the spot. When we do this, we bring the broken and sick of our world to Jesus.

» Pray it: With younger children make a sickness prayer list, include people at church or children at school. Invite the children to pray for others.

Weed: When did you see someone broken, or sick, or hurting today? Did you pray for them? Did you tell them you prayed for them? How did it turn out?

Thursday

Till: You are the Master Gardener. You know exactly how to grow the souls of human beings. Help us to work with you.

Plant: Mark 7:1-23

Water:

» Pick it: This is a great conversation to have in a garden. If you don't have one, consider visiting an orchard, or check your newspaper for a "you pick" patch of some sort. As you are picking talk about how raspberry bushes make raspberries; they can't make anything else. But they can't make raspberries unless they get lots of water and sun and are planted in good soil. It's the same with the human heart. Human hearts have to be planted in good soil. And we water them with love from God and love from each other. The stories of the Bible feed our hearts, and the warmth of prayer is like the sun. When our hearts get what they need they grow the good fruits of love and kindness.

» Draw it: Invite everyone to participate and draw a heart planted in good soil, being properly cared for. Tape it to the bathroom wall to remind everyone of the potential of each day.

Weed: When did you take care of your heart today? What did you do? Where did you see goodness today?

Friday

Till: Lord Jesus, you were always ready to help where you were needed. Help us to be ready as well.

Plant: Mark 7:24-37

Water:

» Act it: Assign parts and act these scenes out.

» Prepare for it: Jesus was always ready to help people when they needed it. What are some things that you can do to be ready when people need help? (Examples: Watch, pray, listen to the Holy Spirit, set some money aside each month and pray for discernment when to use it, keep a simple family schedule so that when someone is in need you can help, be flexible.)

Weed: When today did you see someone in need? What did you do? Was there a time today that you were in need? Did someone help you?

Saturday

Till: Lord, sometimes the problems of the world seems so large that we don't know what we can do to help. In fact sometimes the problems in our homes make us want to give up and say with the disciples, "What do you expect us to do about it?" Remind us that you don't ask us to do it ourselves; instead you invite us to work with you.

Plant: Mark 8:1-10

Water:

» Solve it: When we read the newspaper to pray for others, we can become so overwhelmed by all the needs that we do nothing. We don't have to "eat the whole pie," or solve the whole problem. Instead, we can take one small bite, working with God in consistent small ways to spread his love and goodness.

» Discuss it: Share a problem or need that keeps coming to your mind. In what ways do you think God is asking you to take a small bite?

Weed: When did you see needs today? What small thing did you do to spread the love and goodness of God?

Week of Sunday closest to August 3

Sunday

Till: Your people were looking for the Messiah. When Philip found you he was overjoyed. Help us to look for you today.

Plant: John 1:43-51

Water:

» Seek him: Play "Hide and Seek." Even if your older children don't want to play, insist on it. They will have more fun than they think. I (Lacy) have seen a teenage boy squeeze himself into the wheel of a Papasan chair—the best part was watching his family help him get out! After the fun, invite everyone to talk about the similarities the game and looking for Jesus. When we look do we expect to find him?

» Find him: What are the ways you can look for Jesus today? Examples: In kindness from others, seeing someone forgive, a celebration, waiting patiently.

Weed: When did you look for Jesus today? Where did you find him?

Monday
· · · · · · · ·

Till: Lord Jesus, thank you for warning us. Help us to listen and learn from your life. Protect our minds and hearts from the lies people tell about you.

Plant: Mark 8:11-21

Water:

> » Color it: Fill a glass of water. Tell the children, this glass of water is like Jesus. He came and showed us what God is really like. But we have to be careful: people may tell us that God is mean, or that he doesn't love us. We have to close our ears, because it is not true. (Put a few drops of food coloring into the glass, and slowly stir.) If we listen to the lies of others about God, our pure water isn't pure anymore.

> » Rethink it: As Trevor Hudson explains in the first chapter of his book, *Discovering Our Spiritual Identity*, Jesus shows us what God is like. God is Christ-like. Think about your thinking. Discuss as a family what you think about God. Is he like Jesus? If not, your thinking maybe wrong.

Weed: When did you give or receive love today?

Tuesday
· · · · · · · · ·

Till: Thank you, Jesus, for coming to Earth in a human body and showing us what God is really like. Help us to think rightly about you.

Plant: Mark 8:22-33

Water:

> » Hunt it: In this passage Peter thinks that Jesus will rule as a king and never be killed. He thinks that Jesus will tell everyone what to do and whip them into shape. But that is not his way; it is not God's way. Jesus leads by suffering; he lives by dying. Send everyone on a scavenger hunt around the house. Have them collect as many things as possible

that are opposites and bring them to a central location. Discuss the opposite-ness of the objects.

> » Watch it: As you go through your day today, watch for the ways that God is opposite of the world.

Weed: What gave you joy or sorrow today? Tell these things to God, then pause and imagine God's love flowing all over you.

Wednesday
. . . .

Till: Jesus, not only are you God's Son, but you are the best teacher ever! You taught us so much about God and about how to live in God's kingdom. Help us to be good students.

Plant: Mark 8:34 - 9:1

Water:

> » Follow it: With younger children, play "Follow the Leader." Take turns being the leader. After playing, talk about how Jesus is our leader and we follow him. What are some of the things he leads us to do? How can we do them today?

> » Think it: Here is another chance to think about our thinking. What is Jesus telling us about God? What does that say about how we are to be? Does your thinking need to be changed?

Weed: Where did you follow Jesus today? Did you see any false thinking about God today? What are you the most grateful or least grateful for?

Thursday

Till: Even your disciples who were right there with you had questions. Thank you, Jesus, for being a good teacher. You patiently help us to understand and follow you. We love you.

Plant: Mark 9:2-13

Water:

» Draw it: Invite the children to draw this scene. Hang it in a place where everyone can see it, such as on the refrigerator. Let it be a reminder that Jesus is God's Son.

» Ask him: God is big enough for our questions. They don't make him angry. The disciples had questions and they asked Jesus. What questions do you have? Discuss these questions with your family. We may not know the answers to those questions. The worst thing we can do is make up answers or pretend to know when we don't. Instead take those questions to Jesus, asking and patiently waiting for him to answer. He is a good teacher.

Weed: What did you learn from Jesus today? Did Jesus answer any of your questions? How did he do it? (Examples: Through a Bible reading, through the words of another, a still small voice you heard coming from your heart.)

Friday

Till: There are so many ways that we can follow you, but sometimes we struggle to believe. Our minds want to, but our heart doesn't follow. Help us believe; Lord Jesus, only you can change our hearts.

Plant: Mark 9:14-29

Water:

» Act it: Invite a family member to read this aloud. Invite people to choose parts and act it out. Afterward discuss who you were in the story, and why they did what they did.

» Ask it: We can't make ourselves really believe something. Belief is a gift from God. What do you struggle to believe today? Ask Jesus to change your heart so that you DO really believe. (Example: Maybe you don't believe that God really loves you, or that God has your best interest in mind, or that God is good.)

Weed: Where did your unbelief show up today? Tell Jesus about this, then pause and imagine the love of God flowing all over you.

Saturday

Till: Jesus, you are so patient and good. When we are wrong, you don't scold us or call us names. Instead you patiently help us to understand. Help us to be like you.

Plant: Mark 9:30-41

Water:

» Sculpt it: Invite younger children to use Silly Putty to sculpt an image of themselves with Jesus. You could also pick up clay at a craft store that will harden, and after the sculpture has hardened, display it in a place where your children can be reminded that they have a special place with Jesus.

» Think it: Again Jesus corrects the faulty thinking of the disciples. What new thing is he teaching them? Is it new to you? Do you need to re-think your thinking about God, again?

Weed: Did you see people today who looked like the least but you knew were the greatest? Have you ever wanted to be first, but found out you were last? Have you ever been last and found out you were first?

Week of Sunday closest to August 10

Sunday

Till: Jesus, you are the light of the world. You have all the power, and you give us as much as we can safely handle. You are not stingy; you do not keep things for yourself. You are generous and good. Help us to follow in your example.

Plant: John 3:22-36

Water:

» Picture it: Gather the family around your wedding photo album. If you don't have one, borrow your parents', or a friend's. (This can be a difficult exercise if hearts are hurting. In the marriage between us and God, it is God's perfect design to love us forever, to commit to stay with us no matter what. Please, do not let God's perfect love for us bring guilt and condemnation, when compared to the imperfect union of human beings.) Talk about how God intended marriage to be a commitment of love. Our Bible reading today paints a picture of how God promises to love us and stick with us no matter what, and how he wants to work with us to build a good life that lasts forever.

» Grow it: As parents our faith is passed on to our children. In order for that faith to grow and to be a lasting faith; it must separate from our influence. We must directly connect our children to Christ, and then let go. Read through the passage several times today and pray, asking Jesus to show you where you need to let go, connecting each child in your care more directly to Christ.

Weed: When did you give or receive love today? When did you feel the most or least free?

Monday
. . . .

Till: Jesus, you are serious about living a holy life. You teach us that following you isn't just a hobby, like soccer or painting. Following you is our life. Help us to understand this.

Plant: Mark 9:42-50

Water:

>» Make peace in it: Tell about a time when you didn't make peace. What could you have done differently? Tell about a time when you saw people fighting: is there anything you could have done to help make peace? What does the absence of peace have to do with our not getting our way?

>» Confess it: Why do you think God is serious about holiness? Holiness is the very best way to live our lives. When we choose to do right we have peace and joy. Think through this by choosing any sin and thinking through the consequences. (Example: Envy is wanting something that isn't ours. We think about that thing all the time. We want it, and we are not happy until we get it. We often treat others badly so we can get it. When we do finally get it, we aren't happy, because we want something else.) Is the person who has sinned in that way happy? How about joyful, peaceful? Is that really the good life? Take fifteen minutes to write in your journal. Find a blank page and write down the sins you need to talk to Jesus about. Talk with him about them. Ask him to forgive you and help you to walk away from them. Tear the paper out and throw it in the trash.

Weed: Tell about a time today when you made peace. Are there sins you need to talk with Jesus about from today? Ask for his help.

Tuesday

Till: Jesus, you gave us perfect pictures. You gave us a perfect picture of how God loves us, and a perfect picture of how to love you. Help us to see them clearly.

Plant: Mark 10:1-16

Water:

» Simple it: What is the kingdom of God? Invite everyone to share the simplest answer they know. (Example: Living my life with God, Jesus, and the Holy Spirit.)

» Marry it: How is life with God like the marriage that Jesus describes? Reread those verses.

Weed: How did you live in God's kingdom today? What would life look like if you were married to Jesus? What gave you joy or sorrow today?

Wednesday

Till: You are so loving. Even when we don't understand and we have trouble following you, you love us. Jesus, help us love you back.

Plant: Mark 10:17-31

Water:

» Think it: Again Jesus teaches about the kingdom of God. He challenges us to think about our thinking. He reminds us that all we think we know is reversed! Reread today's passage; what in your thinking needs to be rethought? (Did you think you could follow God by yourself? Did you think that money would make you happy, or safe? Did you think Jesus wouldn't love you if he saw your heart?)

» Marry it: Reread this passage, thinking about how we are married to God. If we love money more than we love God, what have we done? Are there things that you love more than God? How do we know if we love something?

Weed: What are your new thoughts about God and his kingdom? Tell Jesus about these new thoughts, then pause and imagine God's love pouring all over you.

Thursday

Till: Like a good father, you prepared your disciples for what was coming. You loved them so much you taught them. Jesus, you taught them with your actions to love and serve others.

Plant: Mark 10:32-45

Water:

» Serve it: We know that the kingdom of God is opposite of the kingdom of the world. We know that in order to be first, we have to be last. We know that to demonstrate this, Jesus served others. How can you serve others today? Start with the people in your family: secretly choose one person and serve them today.

» Shush it: When we serve others we want to do it secretly. If we serve others so we can be praised and told how great we are, we really didn't serve them, we served ourselves. Come up with a whole family secret service that you can do this week. Keep it a family secret. (Example: Covertly shovel or sweep the neighbor's walkway.)

Weed: How did your secret service go today? How did it feel to be served? Continue planning your whole family secret service. When did you feel the most or least free today?

Friday

Till: God, you are not our divine butler. You do not just grant our wishes. You are our Father and you give us our requests if they are good for us. Help us to ask you for what we need.

Plant: Mark 10:46-52

Water:

> » Act it: Invite the family to act this out, assigning the part of Jesus to the youngest child.

> » Ask it: What do you need? God is a good father and will give us what we need. (He knows what is best for us, and will give us that. Sometimes not giving us what we want is the best for us.)

Weed: When did you give or receive love today?

Saturday

Till: Jesus, we worship you. You teach us. You listen to us. You love us. You are patient with us. You give us what we need. You are what we need. We love you.

Plant: Mark 11:1-11

Water:

> » Sing it: Give each person a chance to share all that they have learned about God through the life of Jesus. Sing and/or dance your thankfulness. Play a praise CD and sing along.

» Celebrate it: Plan a family party celebrating the life of Jesus this week.

Weed: How did you worship and praise God throughout the day? Continue in your party planning. What gave you joy or sorrow today?

Week of Sunday closest to August 17

Sunday

Till: Jesus you are the light of the world. You have all the power, and you give us as much as we can safely handle. You are not stingy; you do not keep things for yourself. You are generous and good. Help us to follow in your example.

Plant: John 5:30-47

Water:

» Teamwork it: Jesus explains how he and God work together. They are perfectly tuned to one another. How does working together better than working alone? How can you work with others today?

» Plug into it: How do we receive life from Jesus? What are some ways to "plug in?" (Examples: Serve others, pray, listen, read the Bible, look for Jesus throughout the day.)

Weed: How did you work with others today? How did you plug into Jesus today? When did you feel the most free or least free?

Monday

Till: God, your kingdom is our whole lives lived with you. Help us to understand that this is not an extra part to life, but our whole life. Thank you for helping us know the seriousness of the matter.

Plant: Mark 11:12-26

Water:

» Embrace it: Practice hugging. Give a half hug, like the person is stinky. Then give a hug like you haven't seen the other person in a long time. Give a big family bear hug. Talk about how we can open our arm wide and pull the kingdom of God fully into ourselves, like a big bear hug.

» Pray it: What would you pray for if you embraced the kingdom of God in a big bear hug? What would your prayers be like if you embraced the kingdom of God in a stinky half hug? Today pray the bear hug prayers.

Weed: What drew you to God today? What drew you away from God today?

Tuesday

Till: We are your farmhands. You trust us, and have given us what we need to take care of your gardens. Help us to be responsible.

Plant: Mark 11:27 - 12:12

Water:

» Act it: Assign parts and act out Mark 12:1-12. What is the garden that God has put you in charge of? (Everyone has a garden: school, work, etc.) Jesus shows us the best way to work those gardens. How are you doing? How do you treat the Son when he comes to help you out?

» Control it: Reread Mark 11:27-33. How do the leaders try to control the people? They don't respond out of honesty; instead they use their words to control others. Today, think about the way you talk to people.

Do you respond honestly or do you try to control people? How does Jesus respond?

Weed: When did you experience kindness or gentleness today?

Wednesday

Till: Jesus, you always speak with honesty. You never try to control us. Instead you are truthful, and loving. Help us to be the same.

Plant: Mark 12:13-27

Water:

> » Recognize it: The leaders are at it again, trying to control. Discuss the signs that we might be trying to control people. (Examples: Talking before listening, interrupting, having our mind made up before we have heard the other person.)

> » Speak it: What are some ways we can speak without trying to control others? (Examples: Be only one side of the conversation. Don't try to imagine or force the other person to say what you want.)

Weed: When did you feel the most free or least free?

Thursday

Till: Jesus you are the best teacher. You help us to understand God's kingdom in a simple way. Thank you for loving us this way.

Plant: Mark 12:28-34

Water:

- » Draw it: Invite the younger members to draw an example of the two commandments. Place it in a prominent place for a reminder.

- » Love him: Jesus says the first commandment is to love God. Reread verses 29-30. Do you love God this way? Be honest, tell Jesus and ask for his help.

- » Love Them: Jesus says the second commandment is to love others. Reread verse 31. Do you love others this way? Be honest, tell Jesus and ask for his help.

Weed: What drew you to God today? What drew you away from God today?

Friday
......

Till: God, you are the great giver. You always give extravagantly. Help us to follow your example.

Plant: Mark 12:35-44

Water:

- » Think it: Once again, Jesus challenges us to think about our thinking. Do we think that the person who gives the most is the holiest? Do we think that religious people are the best people? What does Jesus say?

- » Give it: Why we give is important. Are we giving because we think we have to? Or are we giving because we want to? Ask Jesus to help you with this.

Weed: What gave you joy or sorrow today?

Saturday

Till: God, you are so good. You sent Jesus and showed us what you are like. Through Jesus we can know you so well that others can't trick us. Help us to stick close to you.

Plant: Mark 13:1-13

Water:

» Recognize it: Place a piece of plastic fruit among real fruit of the same kind. Invite children to choose the fake. Try to trick them. Tell the children: Over and over again, we've talked about Jesus helping us to know what God is like. There are many people who say they speak for God. How can we know if they tell the truth? We watch them, and see if their life is like Jesus. If we know the real thing, it's easy to spot a fake.

» Race it: Set up a family running race. Include starting line and finish line celebrations. During the party discuss how Jesus encourages us to stay with the kingdom of God. We won't be sorry: like with the race, it's not about winning but about running, doing the best you can, and crossing that line at the end. (Alternatively, your family can sign up for a charity 5K. They are very positive environments; your family can run or walk. The goal is the same: keep moving forward and cross that line. Be sure to have a celebration!)

Weed: What drew you to God today? What drew you away from God today?

Week of Sunday closest to August 24

Sunday

Till: Jesus, you are the world's light. When we follow you, we are in the light too. Help us to shine your light so others can see.

Plant: John 8:12-20

Water:

» Light it: Eat dinner by candlelight. Talk about today's passage, about how Jesus is the world's light. Discuss what it would be like to eat without light. When we follow Jesus we live in the light; if we don't we stumble around in the darkness.

» Shine it: Turn the lights off in the house. Give the youngest child a flashlight and invite him/her to lead you on a tour of the house. While you are all following, talk about shining the light of Jesus for others. How do we do that? We serve them. We listen to them. We pray for them.

Weed: Where did you see the light of Jesus today? When did you shine the light of Jesus today?

Monday

Till: Lord Jesus, you are the Messiah. Help us to know you so well that we don't worry about being tricked by others. Remind us that we can trust you.

Plant: Mark 13:14-27

Water:

> » Know him: God is love. The best way to know if something is a fake is to know the real thing. Take time to look up and read these verses: 1 John 4:8, 1 Corinthians 13:4-13. Meditate on them; let them sink into your heart. This is what God is like. When you hear someone say that they speak for God, think about these verses.

> » Compare it: Locate some play money, perhaps from a board game. Invite the children to look at it and talk about its characteristics. Now pull out some real money. Compare the two. Talk about the differences, about how real money can buy food and clothes but fake can't do much.

Weed: What drew you to God today? What drew you away from God today?

Tuesday

Till: Jesus, help us to keep watching. Help us to follow you and not fall away. We can trust you to hold on to us.

Plant: Mark 13:28-37

Water:

> » Pack it: Grab several pieces of luggage (or backpacks), for each member of the family. Tell everyone that you are going on a trip and to pack only what is necessary. While they are doing that set up an obstacle course, making it shorter and less complicated for younger people, longer and more complicated for older people. Invite everyone to run

the obstacle course with their luggage. After "running your race," run it again this time without the luggage.

> » Leave it: Talk about how easy it was to run the race without the luggage. Think of things that drag you down or trip you up in life. How can you leave those things behind?

Weed: When did you feel the most or least free today?

Wednesday
....

Till: Lord Jesus, we love you and we worship you. We want to show you just how much we love you. Help us to know how, and to have the courage to do it.

Plant: Mark 14:1-11

Water:

> » Love him: The woman with the perfume loved Jesus very much and wanted to show him just how much. Think about how much you love Jesus. What can you do today to show him? (Examples: Write a poem, paint a picture, sing a song, create a dance.)

> » Worship him: Thankfulness is the seed of worship. When we think about all we are thankful for we naturally begin to worship. Together voice prayers of thankfulness.

Weed: When did you give or receive love today? What are you most grateful for today?

Thursday

Till: Lord Jesus, you are always prepared. You were getting things ready for the Passover meal since the beginning of time. We want to prepare with you. Help us to work with you.

Plant: Mark 14:12-26

Water:

» Prepare it: Plan to prepare dinner tonight as a family. Make it a special dinner. Plan to act out today's Scripture during dinner. Talk about the preparations; give each person a special job to do.

» Work it: During dinner talk about how special the Passover dinner was. Talk about the Eucharist (Communion) and how special it is to Christians. Then talk about how Jesus didn't prepare it alone; he asked his disciples to help. He wants to work with us. What are some ways you can work with Jesus on something special?

Weed: When were you aware of God's presence today? Tell God about these times, then pause and imagine the love of God pouring out all over you.

Friday

Till: Jesus, you know that when life gets tough we need you. You taught us to pray, to come to you no matter what. Help us to come to you during the easy times and the tough times.

Plant: Mark 14:27-42

Water:

» Pray it: Jesus asked his disciples to pray over and over so that they would stay strong. When do you find it hard to pray? When you are happy, sad, or busy? Invite each family member to share.

» Share it: Sometimes we can't pray and God knows that. He created us to support each other and one way is through prayer. When we can't pray, we can share our concern with another person and they can pray for us. Share your concerns with one another and pray.

Weed: When did you experience faithfulness and joy today? When were you aware of God's presence?

Saturday

Till: Jesus, You know what it's like to love someone who doesn't love you back. You know what it's like when a friend hurts you. Help us to remember and come to you when we are hurt.

Plant: Mark 14:43-52

Water:

» Tell it: Jesus knows what it's like to love someone when they don't love you back. Tell about a time you have loved someone and they didn't love you. (This can be an especially tender time for teenaged children; a sympathetic and listening ear is needed.)

» Forgive it: Even though all of Jesus friends left him, he forgave them. He still loved and didn't hate. How can you forgive those who have hurt you? We know we have forgiven someone when we hope the best for them. Talk about forgiveness and boundaries; often loving someone who has hurt us includes not letting them hurt us again.

Weed: Hold in your mind those who love you, then pause and give those people to Jesus. Hold in your mind those who have hurt you, then pause and give those people to Jesus. Pause one last time and imagine God's love pouring all over you.

Week of Sunday closest to August 31

Sunday

Till: Lord Jesus, help us to know the difference between the truth and lies. Help us to walk so closely with you that we never believe the lies. We love you and need you.

Plant: John 8:42-59

Water:

» List it: Make a list of things people believe about God that aren't true, and a list of things that are true. How can we know these are true? Let's teach our children to use the brains God has given them. If you don't know the answer to a truth about God, go searching for it. "Just because" is rarely a good answer.

» Think it: What do you think about God? Is he Christ-like? If you have been using Good Dirt for the last year, then as a family you have read and reread the gospels. Ask your mind and heart: is God Christ-like?

Weed: When did you feel the most or least free today? Where did you experience goodness?

Monday
. . . .

Till: Jesus, they treated you so badly. Our hearts are sad that you were beaten. Help us to remember the violence that you suffered for us.

Plant: Mark 14:53-65

Water:

- » Draw it: Imagine verse 62, and then draw it.

- » Feel it: Reread the passage. Jesus is being abused. Because children are new to violence, they will feel the sadness more greatly than adults. Invite them to share how this makes them feel. Talk with them about the poison of violence: violence begets violence.

Weed: When did you experience gentleness and peace today? When were you worried? Tell Jesus about these, then pause and imagine the love of God pouring all over you.

Tuesday
. . . .

Till: Oh Jesus, so many times we are like Peter. We promise to follow you, but we get lost. You loved Peter even when he denied you. Help us to remember that.

Plant: Mark 14:66-72

Water:

- » Confess it: Jesus and Peter were best friends. In this passage Peter denies he ever knew Jesus. How do you think Jesus felt? How do you think Peter felt? Sometimes we also act like Peter. When we don't share our things or when we must have our way, we act like we don't know Jesus. Jesus still loves us and forgives us. Pray together as a family, confessing when you have denied Jesus. Pronounce the forgiveness of Jesus to each other, saying, "Jesus loves you and forgives you."

» Mean it: Sometimes we say we are sorry when we don't mean it. Re-read verses 71-72. Do you think Peter was sorry about what he did? How do you know? It's important to tell the truth. If we know we should be sorry, but we are not, we should ask Jesus to help us understand the hurt our actions caused. Talk about this as a family, then pray with those who are struggling.

Weed: What drew you close to God today? What drew you away from God today?

Wednesday
. . . .

Till: God, help us to be strong and truthful even when those around us are not. Help us to walk so closely with you that we don't notice the crowds.

Plant: Mark 15:1-12

Water:

» Walk it: People are all around us. Some people walk with God and others don't. In fact we're often around people who do not walk with God. We become like the people we're around. How can we continue to walk with God when others around us do not?

» Don't Do It: It was the crowds of people that wanted to kill Jesus? Do you think there was anyone in crowd that didn't want him to be killed? Why do you think they didn't speak up? Have you ever been in a situation similar to this; where a crowd of people wanted to do something you didn't? What did you do?

Weed: How did you walk with God today? If you were around crowds of people today, did you watch how they behaved? Where did you experience God's presence today?

Thursday

Till: Jesus, every part of your life shows us how to live. You even showed us how to live, when you died.

Plant: Mark 15:11-21

Water:

» Release it: Jesus showed us how to live when he died. When he went to the cross he showed us how to let go of getting our way. Reread verse 21. What is your cross today? Where do you need to let go of getting your way?

» Write it: This is a very sad scene. One of the best ways to express emotion is through poems. Many of the Psalms are emotionally loaded poems. Reread today's scripture and invite the family to spend 15 minutes to 30 minutes writing a poem about it. When the time is up, keep your poem with you and work on it as you have time.

Weed: When did you let go of having to get your way? When did you insist on your way? When did you feel the most or least free?

Friday

Till: Jesus, you know the power of words. You used your words to heal and encourage and love. Others used their words to kill and hurt you. Help us to follow you and use our words as you did.

Plant: Mark 15:22-32

Water:

» Say it: Jesus used his words to give life. How can you do the same today?

» List it: Words can kill. What are some ways that people use words to hurt others? Make a list of words that hurt. (Examples: Shut up. I don't care. I hate you.) There are strong emotions behind these words. How can we express the emotions without hurting people we love?

Weed: How did you use words today? Did anyone use their words to hurt or help you today? Tell about it.

Saturday
. . . .

Till: Jesus, even you felt like God left you. Sometimes we feel alone; remind us that you are always with us. We are never alone.

Plant: Mark 15:33-39

Water:

» Don't fear it: Fear comes from thinking that we are alone. Tell about a time when you were afraid because you thought you were alone. Small children often struggle with bedtime because they are afraid to be alone. Talk about how God is always with us. Talk about how Jesus knows what it is like to feel alone, that we can talk to him about it.

» Hold it: Go for a walk today. Take the time to choose a small rock that will fit in the palm of your hand and in your pocket. Invite each person to carry their rock throughout the day, letting it be a reminder that God is with us and we are never alone.

Weed: Tell about a time when you remembered that God was with you. Tell about a time when you were afraid today.

Week of Sunday closest to Sept 7

Sunday

Till: God, we want to see you. We want to know what you are like. Help us to see you in your Son, Jesus. Help us to know that you are Christ-like.

Plant: John 10:31-42

Water:

» Picture it: Grab the family photo album. Notice how much each generation looks like the last. Help you children to pick out ways they look like you. Jesus also "looked like" his Father. God is in Jesus and Jesus is in him, in the same way that your dad's brown eyes are in you and your big feet are in him.

» Act it: Talk about your actions. What things do you do that your parents do? What sayings do you say? What mannerisms are you passing on? (I (Lacy) am from four generations of hair twisters, usually when we get tired.) Jesus was always forgiving people and accepting them into his company. His Father is just like that. He was always forgiving people and accepting them into his company. God is your Father too. In what ways do you see him in you?

Weed: In what ways did you see God in yourself today? In what ways did you see God in others today?

Monday
. . . .

Till: Jesus, show us how we can serve you. Show us where we need to act without having to be asked. Thank you for the example of Joseph, the wonderful man who buried your body.

Plant: Mark 15:40-47

Water:

> »   Plant it: Jesus did not tell Joseph to bury his body. Joseph knew it was something that needed to be done and he did it. God doesn't always ask us specifically to do things. Most often he wants us to "just do it." What are some things that need to be done today, without your being asked?

> »   Do it, quietly: Try to do the things on your list without being told and without making a big deal out of it. Joseph did not make a big deal out of burying Jesus; he just did what needed to be done.

Weed: What did you do today that needed to be done? Did anyone have to ask you? When did you experience kindness today?

Tuesday
. . . .

Till: Jesus, you brought us the kingdom of God and the best good news, ever! Help us to show others that good news with our lives.

Plant: Mark 16:1-20

Water:

> »   Act it: Act out today's scripture reading. Act it out again, stopping with verse 8. Discuss which version you like best and why.

> »   Tell it: What is the message of God's good news? How can you live that message today, without using words?

Weed: When today, did you think about the message of God's good news? When today, did you live the message of God's good news without using words? What gave you joy or sorrow today?

Wednesday

Till: God, you had a plan for your Son from the very beginning. Help us to remember that you have a plan for us too, even from our very beginning.

Plant: Matthew 2:1-12

Water:

» Act it: Assign parts and act out this section of scripture.

» Draw it: Invite everyone to draw verse 12. While drawing talk about what it might have been like to have had this dream. Ask God to speak to you in your dreams.

Weed: What drew you to God today? What drew you away from God today? Ask God to speak to you through your dreams tonight. If you feel comfortable, share your dreams at breakfast in the morning.

Thursday

Till: God, you have often spoken to people through dreams. And you still do today. Help us to listen and look even when we are asleep.

Plant: Matthew 2:13-23

Water:

» Dream it: Make a Dream Collage. Reread this section of scripture. Give each person a piece of paper, inviting them to draw the dreams. Talk about how we don't have to make up dreams, or say that God spoke to us when he did not. It doesn't mean that God loves us more if he speaks to us through a dream. Sometimes, though, he does talk to us through our dreams, and that is good too. Each one can share about a time when God spoke to them in a dream, if that has happened.

» Think it: Reread the section in the Series Introduction on helping children hear from God. Invite the children to talk through the process of discerning whether it was God speaking to them.

Weed: When did you hear God speak to you today? Ask God to speak to you through your dreams tonight. At breakfast share your dreams.

Friday
......

Till: Jesus, only you can help us make our roads smooth and straight. We can't change our lives by ourselves. Help us to get ready for you.

Plant: Matthew 3:1-12

Water:

» Play it: Locate some toy cars or trucks. Go outside together and make a small dirt road, or mark off a space on the sidewalk. Take a few rocks and put them in the road. Now, invite the children (or adults who are child-like, which is good) to race the cars on the road. Talk about the obstacles, and then remove the obstacles.

» Discuss it: Talk about the words of John the Baptist. He said to make the road to Jesus smooth and straight. Why would we want a road to be smooth and straight? John said that in order to make the road smooth and straight people had to change their lives. What do you think that means?

Weed: When did you make your life road smooth and straight today? What obstacles did you remove? Tell about something good that happened today.

Saturday

Till: Jesus, you were always showing us how to live with God. When you were baptized, you showed us that it all begins with a new life.

Plant: Matthew 3:13-17

Water:

» Act it: Act out this scene. What do you think it means to be baptized? Tell about when you were baptized. Why did you do it and what did it mean to you?

» Remember it: Grab a small bowl of water. Some Christian traditions practice marking each other with the Sign of the Cross using water as an outward reminder that God is with us and we belong to him. Gather around one family member. Dip your finger in the water, and make the sign of the cross on that person's forehead. Say, "You are God's beloved child. You belong to him and he will take care of you." Move around the family circle, until each person has been marked by love.

Weed: When did you think about being baptized today? If there is someone in your family who would like to be baptized, talk to your pastor about the details. When were you aware of the presence of God today?

Week of Sunday closest to Sept 14

....

Sunday
·······

Till: Thank you, Jesus, for showing us what God is like. Thank you for not changing to make the Pharisees happy.

Plant: John 11:45-57

Water:

» Show it: The Pharisees said that Jesus just kept on "creating God-signs." He just kept on looking like his Father, doing things that only his Father does. What are some things that you can do that God does? (Examples: Forgive others, help others, love others, go last instead of first.)

» Know it: Notice that the Pharisees didn't like Jesus acting like his Father. Jesus reminds us that it will be the same for us. Often when we are forgiving or kind, others will not want us to do that; they may want us to stay angry. Just like Jesus did, we ignore their desire and continue being like our Father in heaven.

Weed: When were you like your Father in heaven today? Where did you experience joy and generosity today?

Monday

Till: Jesus, you prepared for your test by fasting. Help us to know what to fast and when it is good for us to fast. Help us know how to get ready.

Plant: Matthew 4:1-11

Water:

> » Fast it: Fasting is when we give up things for a time so we can hear God better. It is best for children not to fast nutritional food, but they can fast from desserts. Children can also fast from television, or video games. Talk about what it means to fast, and why Jesus fasted. Choose to fast from something for the next week as a family, filling that space with time together reading the scriptures, praying and singing.

> » Give it: Talk about the times in the Bible people fasted because they were in distress. Read Esther 4. What issues in the world today cause us distress? For example, at this writing there is a massive famine in Somalia. As a family, choose something to fast and pray for the distressing issue, asking God to show you what He would have you to do as a family to ease the suffering. This may be as simple as eating beans and corn bread three times a week and sending the money saved to ease suffering.

Weed: Where did you see distress today? Did it make you want to fast? Tell about how it made you feel to give up something you wanted today? When did you experience God's presence today?

Tuesday

Till: Jesus, you challenge us to turn around and follow you. God's kingdom is here. Help us to follow you into the kingdom.

Plant: Matthew 4:12-17

Water:

» Change it: In what way could you change and become more like Jesus? Maybe you could be more kind. Maybe you could have more patience; maybe you could obey your parents. Choose one way and share with your family the way you could be more like Jesus. Take turns praying for one another.

» Live it: The kingdom of God is a perfectly safe place where what God wants to happen, happens. It is a place where all things work together for our good. Are you living in God's kingdom today? Do you trust God to take care of all things? What are you worried about today? Using Silly Putty or clay, sculpt the thing you are most worried about and leave it next to your Bible.

Weed: What gave you joy or sorrow today?

Wednesday

Till: Jesus, help us to follow you like Peter and Andrew. Help us to drop everything and just go.

Plant: Matthew 4:18-25

Water:

» Act it: Reread verses 23-25 then act them out. Take some creative liberty and assign each person an ailment. Invite them to act out how they were before Jesus healed them, while Jesus was healing them, and after Jesus healed them.

» Discuss it: What is the good government of God like? How can you live in it today?

Weed: What drew you near to God today? What drew you away from God today?

Thursday

Till: Lord Jesus, you show us what God's kingdom is like. You show us how it works and how safe it is. Help us to live in it every day!

Plant: Matthew 5:1-10

Water:

> » *For the next week or so, we're going to be reading Jesus' Sermon on the Mount, Matthew 5-7. In it Jesus tells us how to live the very best life there is! He tells us how to live in God's kingdom. Beginning today, have a blank book and colored pencils or crayons or markers on hand. Write on the front of the book, "Kingdom Living." Each day you'll want to have your Kingdom Living book and supplies ready.

> » Think it: Reread today's scripture, and ask, "What does Jesus tell us about God's kingdom?" Discuss this as a family, then choose one or two characteristics of God's kingdom.

> » Write and draw it: Write and draw that characteristic in your book. Be sure to date and label the page.

Weed: When did you experience love, joy, peace or patience today? Did you give these, or received them?

Friday

Till: Lord Jesus, so many people don't know why they are here on earth, but you tell us plainly and clearly that we are the light, just as you are the light. Help us to shine!

Plant: Matthew 5:11-16

Water:

» Think it: Reread today's scripture, and ask, "What does Jesus tell us about God's kingdom?" Discuss this as a family, then choose one or two characteristics of God's kingdom.

» Write and draw it: Write and draw that characteristic in your Kingdom Living book. Be sure to date and label the page.

Weed: When did you see the light of Jesus today? When were you the light of Jesus?

Saturday
....

Till: Jesus, you knew the Old Testament. You knew that the Scriptures were important. Help us to know them and know that they are important.

Plant: Matthew 5:17-20

Water:

» Think it: Reread today's scripture, and ask, "What does Jesus tell us about God's kingdom?" Discuss this as a family, then choose one or two characteristics of God's kingdom.

» Write and draw it: Write and draw that characteristic in your Kingdom Living book. Be sure to date and label the page.

Weed: When did you experience self-control or faithfulness today? When were you aware that God is with you?

Week of Sunday closest to Sept 21

Sunday

Till: Oh Jesus, we need your help! Help us to follow you because we love you, not just because others are following you.

Plant: Luke 3:7-18

Water:

» Tell it: God honors honesty and John knew it. He already knows us and knows why we do things, so we can be sure He will still love us no matter what we tell Him. What are some things you need to be honest about?

» Sculpt it: Sometimes it is hard to be honest out loud. Sculpt the thing you need to be honest about. Holding the thing in your hand, talk to God silently about it. Leave it beside the Bible in God's hands.

Weed: When did you see something that was honest and true today? How did it make you feel?

Monday

Till: Jesus, you taught us that in God's kingdom people matter. Help us to love others like you love others.

Plant: Matthew 5:21-26

Water:

> » Think it: Reread today's scripture, and ask, "What does Jesus tell us about God's kingdom?" Discuss this as a family, then choose one or two characteristics of God's kingdom.

> » Write and draw it: Write and draw that characteristic in your Kingdom Living book. Be sure to date and label the page.

Weed: Where did you see God's kingdom today? When did you live in God's kingdom today?

Tuesday

Till: Jesus, you taught us that in God's kingdom sin is a very serious thing! Sin hurts us and hurts others. Help us to take it as seriously as you do.

Plant: Matthew 5:27-37

Water:

> » Think it: Reread today's scripture, and ask, "What does Jesus tell us about God's kingdom?" Discuss this as a family, then choose one or two characteristics of God's kingdom.

> » Write and draw it: Write and draw that characteristic in your Kingdom Living book. Be sure to date and label the page.

Weed: Where did you see God's kingdom today? When did you live in God's kingdom today?

Wednesday

Till: Jesus, sometimes we forget how we are to treat each other is God's kingdom. Thank you for telling us and showing us.

Plant: Matthew 5:38-48

Water:

> » Think it: Reread today's scripture, and ask, "What does Jesus tell us about God's kingdom?" Discuss this as a family, then choose one or two characteristics of God's kingdom.

> » Write and draw it: Write and draw that characteristic in your Kingdom Living book. Be sure to date and label the page.

Weed: When did you experience kindness and patience today? What is drawing you to God? What is drawing you away from God?

Thursday

Till: Jesus, thank you for teaching us how to pray.

Plant: Matthew 6:1-6

Water:

> » Think it: Reread today's scripture, and ask, "What does Jesus tell us about God's kingdom?" Discuss this as a family, then choose one or two characteristics of God's kingdom.

> » Write and draw it: Write and draw that characteristic in your Kingdom Living book. Be sure to date and label the page.

Weed: Where did you see God's kingdom today? When did you live in God's kingdom today? When were you aware that God was with you?

Friday

Till: Jesus, thank you for showing us how to pray.

Plant: Matthew 6:7-18

Water:

> » Think it: Reread today's scripture, and ask, "What does Jesus tell us about God's kingdom?" Discuss this as a family, then choose one or two characteristics of God's kingdom.

> » Write and draw it: Write and draw that characteristic in your Kingdom Living book. Be sure to date and label the page.

Weed: What are you most or least grateful for today?

Saturday

Till: Jesus, you are so amazing! In your sermon, you teach us that people are more important than things. Help us not to forget that.

Plant: Matthew 6:19-24

Water:

> » Think it: Reread today's scripture and ask, "What does Jesus tell us about God's kingdom?" Discuss this as a family, then choose one or two characteristics of God's kingdom.

> » Write and draw it: Write and draw that characteristic in your Kingdom Living book. Be sure to date and label the page.

Weed: Where did you see God's kingdom today? When did you live in God's kingdom today? When did you give or receive love today?

Week of Sunday closest to Sept 28

....

Sunday

. . . .

Till: Jesus, help us to remember that when we work with you, we get better results than if we work by ourselves.

Plant: Luke 5:1-11

Water:

> » Reflect it: Think about a time when you did something by yourself and it didn't work out. Now think about a time when you worked with God on something. How did it work out?

> » Plan it: Think about this week. When can you work with Jesus, instead of working alone? Invite him to work with you.

Weed: When did you feel the most or least free today?

Monday

Till: Jesus, we live in a world of things. If we don't let you help us, we will begin to worship our things. Help us to remember that people matter more than things.

Plant: Matthew 6:25-34

Water:

» Think it: Reread today's scripture, and ask, "What does Jesus tell us about God's kingdom?" Discuss this as a family, then choose one or two characteristics of God's kingdom.

» Write and draw it: Write and draw that characteristic in your Kingdom Living book. Be sure to date and label the page.

Weed: Where did you see God's kingdom today? When did you live in God's kingdom today? When did you experience goodness today?

Tuesday

Till: Jesus, thank you for making your sermon so easy to understand. Help us to remember to ask ourselves what we want people to do for us, and then do it for them. Anybody can do that!

Plant: Matthew 7:1-12

Water:

» Think it: Reread today's scripture, and ask, "What does Jesus tell us about God's kingdom?" Discuss this as a family, then choose one or two characteristics of God's kingdom.

» Write and draw it: Write and draw that characteristic in your Kingdom Living book. Be sure to date and label the page.

Weed: Where did you see God's kingdom today? When did you live in God's kingdom today? What drew you to God today? What drew you away from God today?

Wednesday

Till: Jesus, you showed us that God loves us. We don't have to try to get his attention, or try to get him to like us. He already does.

Plant: Matthew 7:13-23

Water:

» Think it: Reread today's scripture, and ask, "What does Jesus tell us about God's kingdom?" Discuss this as a family, then choose one or two characteristics of God's kingdom.

» Write and draw it: Write and draw that characteristic in your Kingdom Living book. Be sure to date and label the page.

Weed: Where did you see God's kingdom today? When did you live in God's kingdom today? What gave you joy or sorrow today?

Thursday

Till: Jesus, you showed us exactly what the kingdom of God looks like. You showed us how to live in it. Help us to take your words and live them out!

Plant: Matthew 7:21-29

Water:

» Think it: Reread today's scripture, and ask, "What does Jesus tell us about God's kingdom?" Discuss this as a family, then choose one or two characteristics of God's kingdom.

» Write and draw it: Write and draw that characteristic in your Kingdom Living book. Be sure to date and label the page.

Weed: Where did you see God's kingdom today? When did you live in God's kingdom today? What are you the most or least grateful for?

Friday

Till: Jesus, sometimes we think that you are forced to love us. Sometimes we think that you just put up with us. But that is incorrect. You want to love us; you like us; you want to be with us. We are your beloved.

Plant: Matthew 8:1-17

Water:

» Believe it: We often think wrongly about God. Sometimes we think that he really doesn't want to help us, but, because we're his children, he has to help. Reread verses 1-4. What do they tell us about Jesus? What do they tell us about God?

» Act it: Reread our scripture for today, assign parts and act it out. Switch parts and act it out again. Who in the stories did you most identify with and why?

Weed: When did you experience love and joy today? When did you give or receive goodness?

Saturday

Till: Jesus, help us to remember that when we are with you, no matter what is going on around us, we are safe. Your kingdom is the safest place to be.

Plant: Matthew 8:18-27

Water:

» Sink it: Fill a large bowl or a small tub with water. Cut a paper cup in half lengthwise; this will serve as a boat. Invite the children to draw and cut out paper people. Put the paper cup boat in the water; put the paper people in the cup boat. Reread verses 22-27. Reread it over and over until each child has had the chance to be the storm.

» Discuss it: Tell about a time when you were in a "storm." For children "storms" can often be the first day of school, or going to bed at night. Help the children talk through their storms and show them that Jesus is with them.

Weed: When did you encounter a storm today? How did you know Jesus was with you? When did you feel safe today?

Week of Sunday closest to Oct 5

Sunday

Till: Jesus, you are always with us when we are sad. We never cry alone. Help us to know that you are with us.

Plant: Luke 7:11-17

Water:

> » Act it: Act out the scene, taking turns who gets to be the boy who comes back to life.

> » Tell it: Tell about a time when you were very sad. Ask others to help you see that Jesus was with you. Often Jesus uses human beings to be with us. They love us and hold us like he would if he were there. Tell about a time when someone else was sad, and you were Jesus to them.

Weed: What happened this week that made you feel sad? Tell about how Jesus was with you. Tell about someone you saw this week that was sad, how can you be Jesus to them?

Monday
. . . .

Till: Jesus, you are strong. No one can beat you. Evil spirits are afraid of you. We have nothing to fear when you are with us!

Plant: Matthew 8:28-34

Water:

» Sculpt it: Use Silly Putty and sculpt all the characters in this story while someone rereads the passage. Use your Silly Putty people and pigs to act it out.

» Name it: Invite each person to name things they are afraid of. Talk about each fear and why we can trust Jesus to protect us.

Weed: Tell about a time today when you were afraid. Tell about a time today when you were afraid, but then you remembered that Jesus is with you and it is safe to be with him.

Tuesday
. . . .

Till: Jesus, you can do anything! You can heal our bodies and heal our spirits. Help us to let you do both.

Plant: Matthew 9:1-8

Water:

» Body: What in your body today needs to be healed? Invite your family to pray for you.

» Spirit: What in your spirit needs to be forgiven? Invite your family to pray with you.

Weed: When did you see someone today whose body needs to be healed? When did you see someone today whose spirit needs to be forgiven? Tell Jesus about these people, then pause and imagine that God's love is pouring through you to those who need healing.

Wednesday

Till: Jesus, you knew how to celebrate. The best news ever is that God's kingdom came to earth, and all people—even tax collectors—are invited in! Help us to celebrate too!

Plant: Matthew 9:9-17

Water:

» Plan it: If you have been in Good Dirt the last year, we have been living the gospel of Jesus Christ. We are now well acquainted with the kingdom of God. Now it's time to throw a kingdom of God party. Begin the planning now: assign different people to snacks, entertainment (you might consider reenacting some of the stories you have read), decorations, and invitations.

» List it: Make a list of the ways you have grown over the past year.

Weed: Discuss the plans for your kingdom of God party. How did you grow closer to Jesus today? When were you aware that God is with you?

Thursday

Till: Jesus, you were never in a hurry and you always had time for helping others. Help us to be more like you.

Plant:

Matthew 9:18-26

Water:

» Imagine it: Reread the story aloud. Who are you in the story? Reread it aloud again. Imagine that you are that person. What is your response to Jesus?

» Listen to it: Jesus always had time to listen to people. Today when you are talking with others, try to listen and not talk over people. Tie a string around your pointer finger to remember to listen more than you talk.

Weed: How was your listening today? What did people have to say? If you struggled with talking over others, ask your family to pray for you.

Friday

Till: Jesus, help us to believe the truth about you. Help us to believe it with our bodies.

Plant: Matthew 9:27-34

Water:

» Act it: Act out today's scripture passage.

» Discuss it: If Jesus were to say to you today, "Become what you believe", what would you become?

Weed: When did you experience patience and peace today? When did you give up getting your way? When did you know God was with you?

Saturday

Till: Jesus, you choose twelve harvest hands in the beginning. As we follow you, we also become your harvest hands.

Plant: Matthew 9:35 - 10:4

Water:

> »   Harvest it: Jesus called the twelve disciples to help him love others. But he has also put our names on that list. Think about who God would have you to show the love of Jesus today?

> »   Love it: What are some ways we can show love to others today? Try listening to them, praying for them, helping them, forgiving them.

Weed: Tell about a time today where you showed the love of Jesus? Pray for a person you saw today. When were you aware that God is with you?

Week of Sunday closest to Oct 12

Sunday

Till: Jesus, you are the only one who can forgive our sins, thank you! You have welcomed us back into the family of God, and we are very, very grateful.

Plant: Luke 7:36-50

Water:

» Imagine it: Reread today's scripture passage, and as you do, mentally take the part of one of the characters. Perhaps imagine you are the woman weeping at Jesus' feet, because you know you've ruined your life and need help. Or, maybe you're the Pharisees, shocked at this display. Or are you Jesus, looking with compassion and love on both the sinful woman, and the unloving Pharisee? Share with each other how you think your character felt.

» Enter it: Jesus restores the woman back into relationship with God, and he restores us, too! Have you ever had a time when you did something that made you feel distant from someone, such as a parent or a friend, and they forgave you? How did that feel? How does it feel to know God forgives you?

Weed: Where did you feel God's forgiveness today? When were you like the Pharisees today, unforgiving toward others? Tell Jesus about these times, then pause and imagine the love of God pouring all over you.

Monday
· · · · · · · ·

Till: Oh Jesus, sometimes we make sharing your kingdom into such a big production that it scares us, but you know better. Help us to share you right here, where we are, in simple love and generosity.

Plant: Matthew 10:5-15

Water:

» This week, we're reading another sermon given by Jesus. The last one, the Sermon on the Mount, focused on living in the kingdom. This one is about sharing the kingdom. Get another notebook and write "Kingdom Sharing" on the cover. Each day, have your notebook, pencils and colors ready for you to add a page about what we learn.

» Write and draw it: Reread today's passage, and ask, "What did you learn about sharing God's kingdom with others? Write and draw your answer in your Kingdom Sharing notebook. Don't forget to date the page.

Weed: How did you share God's kingdom with others today? What is drawing you to God? What is drawing you away from God?

Tuesday
· · · · · · · ·

Till: God, sometimes sharing your kingdom is hard. People can turn on us and treat us badly even as we love them! Help us not to quit or cave in. Keep us going!

Plant: Matthew 10:16-23

Water:

> » Write and draw it: Reread today's passage, and ask, "What did you learn about sharing God's kingdom with others? Write and draw your answer in your Kingdom Sharing notebook. Don't forget to date the page.

Weed: How did you share God's kingdom with others today? When did you experience peace and faithfulness today?

Wednesday

Till: God, you're our Father. You care about us down to the last detail. Help us not to be intimidated or afraid as we share your kingdom with others.

Plant: Matthew 10:24-33

Water:

> » Write and draw it: Reread today's passage, and ask, "What did you learn about sharing God's kingdom with others? Write and draw your answer in your Kingdom Sharing notebook. Don't forget to date the page.

Weed: How did you share God's kingdom with others today? When did you give or receive love today?

Thursday

Till: God, as we share your kingdom, help us not to overlook the small things we can do to proclaim your love. Be with us as we start small.

Plant: Matthew 10:34-42

Water:

» Write and draw it: Reread today's passage, and ask, "What did you learn about sharing God's kingdom with others? Write and draw your answer in your Kingdom Sharing notebook. Don't forget to date the page.

Weed: How did you share God's kingdom with others today? When were you aware that God is with you?

Friday
......

Till: Jesus, your kingdom comes with power and helps the needy and weak! Help us to get in on what you're doing in our world.

Plant: Matthew 11:1-6

Water:

» Draw it: Jesus quotes a beautiful passage from the Old Testament that describes what it looks like when God's kingdom comes among us. Create a drawing that celebrates the kingdom based on these verses!

» Get in on it: The kingdom of God is good news for the weak, the poor, the sick, and the sad. They discover that God is on their side, not far away! How can your family get in on what God is doing? Maybe you could visit and love some of the elderly in your community, or provide some food for the homeless, or make cards for some of the sick in your church. Make a plan that you can do in the next week or so.

Weed: Where did you get in on sharing God's kingdom today? How does it make you feel to be part of sharing God's kingdom?

Saturday

Till: Jesus, you opened the door for us to enter the kingdom! Your prophet John declared that you were coming, and you came! Jesus, you're the center of everything!

Plant: Matthew 11:7-15

Water:

» Center it: In Jesus' day, the crowds were really impressed with John the Baptist. But he was pointing, with all the rest of the prophets, toward the one who would bring the kingdom of God to us—Jesus! Everything in the Bible points toward Jesus. Today, as a reminder, put a symbol of Jesus right smack in the center of everything. Get a cross, or a crown, or a picture of Jesus, or even a poster of his name, and put it right where everyone can see it, at the center of an important room in your house. You might even have everyone point at it each time they walk into the room.

» Live it: How could you make Jesus the center of an important activity you have today? Make a specific plan for how you can do this with Jesus, and for Jesus.

Weed: When was Jesus at the center of your life today? When did you feel the most or least free today?

Week of Sunday closest to Oct 19

....

Sunday
·······

Till: Jesus, you have asked us all to be harvest workers. And you told us the best way to do it.

Plant: Luke 10:1-12, 17-20

Water:

» Leave it: Since we are harvest workers too, these words are for us. Ask yourself, "What things keep me from focusing on God's kingdom?" How can you get rid of those things? Maybe you think too much about fashion, or food, and it distracts you from thinking about God. How can you make more simple choices about clothes or food, so that you have time to think about God?

» Draw it: Reread verses 18-20. Draw what you see. How does this make you feel?

Weed: What did you leave behind that keeps you from focusing on God? When did you think about your drawing today? When were you aware of God's presence today?

Monday

Till: Jesus, you know that people can say anything. The truth is in what we do. Help us to not only say we follow you, but to actually do it!

Plant: Matthew 11:16-24

Water:

- » Do it: Reread this section aloud. Tell about a time when someone you know was more talk than action. What are some things you've been talking about, but now need to do?

- » Show it: Tell about a time when you said you were going to do something, but didn't do it. Invite your family to pray for you to become a doer and not just a talker.

Weed: How did you show the love of Jesus today, and not just talk about it? When did you give or receive love today?

Tuesday

Till: Jesus, you are tender and gentle and wise and wonderful. Help us to walk gently into God's kingdom with you.

Plant: Matthew 11:25-30

Water:

- » Listen to it: Invite everyone to get in a comfortable spot. Reread the passage slowly three times. After each time, have each person ask, "Holy Spirit, what do you have to say to me?"

- » Record it: Write or draw what the Holy Spirit said. Write or draw your response to him.

Weed: How did the words from Jesus affect your day? When did you experience goodness and beauty today? Tell Jesus about this, then pause and imagine the love of God pouring out all over you.

Wednesday

Till: Jesus, sometimes we try to make you fit our rules. Help us to remember that you are in charge of everything, even the rules.

Plant: Matthew 12:1-14

Water:

> » Rule it: What are some rules around the house? Are you ever allowed to break the rules? Can Mom and Dad break the rules? Why?

> » Live it: Jesus was always kind. Who do you need to be kind to today? Remember that Jesus was kind to people that were kind, but he was also kind to people who were mean. Who do you need to be kind to today who is not kind to you?

Weed: When did you feel the most or least free today? When were you aware that God was with you?

Thursday

Till: God, you told us about your Son long before he came to earth. Help us to listen with our hearts to the prophet Isaiah.

Plant: Matthew 12:15-21

Water:

» Compare it: Read the description Isaiah gives us about Jesus. Compare what you think about Jesus with this description. Do you need to change your thinking?

» Poster it: Make a poster of Isaiah's description. Try to memorize it as a family. Meditate on the person of Jesus.

Weed: Tell about a time when you thought about Jesus today. What are you most or least grateful for today?

Friday
......

Till: Jesus, help us to always be on your side. Help us to listen to and obey the Holy Spirit.

Plant: Matthew 12:22-32

Water:

» Connect it: Jesus tells the Pharisees that he is connected to God. He shows them how they are not connected to God. Think about your heart today; are you connected to God? If not, how can you connect?

» Disconnect it: Often when we are not connected to God, it is because we are connected to something else. What are you connected to today, that you need to disconnect?

Weed: What were you connected to today? How did your connections affect your day? When did you experience goodness today?

Saturday

Till: Jesus, we worry so much about what we look like, but you tell us that our hearts are what are most important. Help us to remember that.

Plant: Matthew 12:33-42

Water:

» Walk it: Take a nature walk, pointing out to the children how nature follows a pattern: whatever the kind of plant or tree it is, that is what kind of fruit it makes. Tomato plants make tomatoes, not cucumbers. If the tomato plant doesn't get water or food from the sun, it dies. If it is pulled up out of the soil, it dies. Invite the children to point out other plants or trees that follow the same pattern.

» Apply it: Discuss how our lives in God's kingdom are similar to the tomato plant. We must stay rooted in God, we must be fed by the Son, and we must let the Scriptures water us. And when we do, we will make fruit.

Weed: When today did you see nature's pattern? How did you live nature's pattern today?

Week of Sunday closest to Oct 26

Sunday

Till: Jesus, you are a wonderful teacher. You see right through to what matters, and you help us learn how to live with you. Please teach us today!

Plant: Luke 10:25-37

Water:

» Act it: This is a great story to act out. Be sure to include the beginning, when the scholar is questioning Jesus. It's an important part of the story!

» Pray it: Jesus is such a good teacher. He sees right away that the religion scholar needs help to understand God's law of love, and tells him a story that gets to the core of his heart. Instead of worrying about how to define "neighbor", this man needs to be a neighbor. Have each family member write a prayer asking Jesus to teach them what they need to know in order to live with him.

Weed: What did Jesus teach you today? Say a simple prayer of thanksgiving for what you are learning.

Monday

Till: God, help us to make room for you, and then really welcome you in. Help us to listen and obey!

Plant: Matthew 12:43-50

Water:

» Wash it: Jesus' story today is hard for us to understand sometimes, but here's an activity to get the idea across. Give each family member two bowls that need to be washed, and let them wash them really well—so they're ready for food. Then, fill one with dirt and the other with a tasty snack. Which one is better for eating? Jesus is teaching us that we can clean ourselves up to get ready, but then not follow him.

» Obey it: What is one way that Jesus is calling you to obey him today as you make room for him in your life?

Weed: When did you intend to obey Jesus? How did it go? When did you experience faithfulness today?

Tuesday

Till: Jesus, till the soil of our hearts, so that our lives are good soil for your good news to grow!

Plant: Matthew 13:1-9

Water:

» Plant it: In our readings for the next few days, Jesus is all about farming parables. So, act out today's story. Get a very fast-sprouting seed, such as grass, and do like the story: scatter some on the sidewalk, some on gravel or rock, and some in the weeds. Then, get a small pot with good, rich soil and plant some there. Each day this week, water all four and see what happens. (In some climates October is a good time to plant grass seed. In others it is already too cold. If it's already too cold where you are, try this in the house by creating the same conditions in plastic totes or boxes. Think of it as a meeting of science and theology!)

» Till it: How can your heart be like rich, good soil for God's word today? How can you be really listening?

Weed: What drew you to God today? What drew you away from God today?

Wednesday

Till: Jesus, give us God-blessed eyes and God-blessed ears today! Help us to see what we see, to hear what we hear, and to be ready to understand your kingdom.

Plant: Matthew 13:10-17

Water:

» Water it: Be sure to water all four of your seed locations today!

» Look for it: Today, search for God's kingdom. Keep a list running throughout the day of all the places you see God: in a beautiful flower or a mewing kitten; in someone's being kind and generous; or in a quiet moment where you remember he loves you. Today, keep your eyes open!

Weed: Where did you see God's kingdom today? Share your list. What do you think it would be like if you looked for him like this every day?

Thursday

Till: Jesus, give us good soil! Protect us from evil, from losing interest in your kingdom, and from worrying about possessions. Let us grow a harvest beyond our wildest dreams, with you!

Plant: Matthew 13:18-23

Water:

> » Water it: Be sure to water all four of your seed locations today!

> » Draw it: Draw each of the four soils from today's parable, using your real-life seed experiment as a guide.

Weed: Today, which of the four soils did you feel most like? Where was God inviting you to be the good soil?

Friday

Till: Jesus, help us understand life in your kingdom as we listen to your parables.

Plant: Matthew 13:24-30

Water:

> » Water it: Continue watering your four seed experiments. (Though, by now, some of the seeds are probably long dead or gone—but just for emphasis, splash some water where they used to be!)

> » Think it: Jesus' parables aren't easy, but they do get us thinking. They help us get our fingers out of our ears and to open up our eyes, so that we can recognize the kingdom of God around us. So, spend some time today thinking and talking, asking "What might this parable mean?"

Weed: Did you have any more thoughts about Jesus' parable? How does it feel to think about Jesus' stories? When did you experience peace and joy today?

Saturday

Till: More stories, Jesus? Sometimes we wish you'd just tell us what to do. We trust that you're a great teacher, so help us engage with all our hearts and imaginations into your stories, so we can learn.

Plant: Matthew 13:31-35

Water:

» Water it: Last day of watering all four spots! You can keep watering the potted seeds, if you like.

» Imagine it: Take some time to picture each of the stories Jesus tells. What might he be teaching about the kingdom?

Weed: Where did you see the kingdom spreading today? When did you experience the presence of God today?

All Saints' Day (November 1)

Seasonal Fun:

Because it falls on a particular day—November 1—All Saints' Day might be in Week 25 or Week 26. This is a day when Christians remember that we are part of a large body of believers that spans both time and space! Theologians call this the "communion of the saints": we have a family of Christians from all over the world and throughout 2000 years of history. While October 31—Halloween, or All Hallows Eve, the night before All Saints'—gets more attention in our culture we can make All Saints' important in our homes. Here are some ideas for you to try.

» Decorate for All Saints' instead of for Halloween: Instead of spooky cobwebs, skeletons or bats, be creative and put up decorations that focus on God's church throughout the world. Do some research and find some decorations from other cultures. Put up pictures of memorable

Christians from different times and countries. (And yes, you can still give out candy on Halloween if you want—no need to be a spoilsport!)

» Dress up as a famous saint for Halloween: Try St. Francis and St. Claire, or Martin Luther, or Mother Teresa.

» Eat a multi-ethnic dinner celebrating the church: Google some recipes from all over the world. Pray for believers in those countries while you eat their foods.

Till: God, you've made us part of a big family. This family extends throughout the world and the ages. Thank you for making us part of your family! Help us learn from others who know you, too.

Plant: Luke 6:20-26

Water:

» Read it: Today, read a biography of a Christian from a different country or time. The book *Stories of the Saints* by Joyce Denham and Judy Stevens is a great bedtime read, or you may be able to find a brief biography on Wikipedia. You might read about St. Aidan or St. Julian of Norwich. What do you learn from them?

Weed: How does it feel to know you're part of God's big family today? When were you aware that God is with you today?

Week of Sunday closest to Nov 2

Sunday

Till: Jesus, help us today to steep in God's reality. You invite us into life with our Father who takes great care over even our smallest needs. Let us be carefree in the care of God!

Plant: Luke 12:22-31

Water:

» Release it: Make a list of things that you are worried about, or that tend to make you unhappy. What would it be like to let these go and trust God? Make an experiment of releasing these cares.

» Enjoy it: Jesus calls you his dearest friends! What worries can you leave with Jesus so that you can just enjoy your day? Think up one worry to leave with him, just for the sheer happiness doing so will bring you and your loved ones. Then do it as a friend of Jesus!

Weed: What was it like being a friend of Jesus today? What was it like trusting God today? When did you give or receive love today?

Monday

Till: Jesus, thank you for explaining the kingdom to us. You give us pictures to prod us and provoke us to thought, but you also tell us plainly what we need to know. You are our Great Teacher!

Plant: Matthew 13:36-43

Water:

» Remember it: Do you remember when we read the parable Jesus is explaining, Matthew 13:24-30? If not, you might go back and reread it. Does his explanation match what you thought he might have meant?

» Draw it: Jesus is telling us a scene from the final act—a picture of what will happen in the end. He tells us that God will root out everything wrong and evil from the world so that those who live in his kingdom will be set free. Draw the scene, illustrating some part of Jesus' words that captures your imagination.

Weed: How do you think it will feel when Jesus comes and saves the world from all that is wrong and evil? Tell Jesus about these feelings, then pause and imagine God's love pouring all over you.

Tuesday

Till: Jesus, life with you in your kingdom—what a find! There is nothing worth more! We would give up anything to get you!

Plant: Matthew 13:44-52

Water:

» Imagine it: What do you think Jesus is telling us about the kingdom of God in these stories?

» Seek it: Play a game based on these parables: hide a prize or candy somewhere in the house, and let the kids find it together. While everyone gets to enjoy the prize, discuss what makes God's kingdom such a great find.

Weed: When did you seek God and his kingdom today? What gave you joy or sorrow today?

Wednesday

Till: Jesus, sometimes we take those we love for granted. Help us to recognize the ways you are with us through our closest friends and loved ones.

Plant: Matthew 13:53-58

Water:

» List it: Just as Jesus' relatives and neighbors couldn't see him for who he was, sometimes we overlook the blessing that our loved ones are to us. Make a list of the ways God blesses you through each member of your family.

» Celebrate it: Think of a creative way you could share with each person in your family what they mean to you. You could make a card, prepare a favorite meal, or find some wildflowers. Be sure to share your list of blessings with them!

Weed: What was it like recognizing the gifts that your family members are to you? How did it feel to be recognized? When did you give or receive love today?

Thursday

Till: God, sometimes such bad things happen to your people. Help us to trust you and come to you with our sorrow and pain.

Plant: Matthew 14:1-12

Water:

> » Mourn it: This is a very sad story of how wicked people can be to one another. Give children a chance to express how this story makes them feel.

> » Pray it: Turn those feelings into a prayer. Perhaps there is a grief in your own family right now, or maybe you know of a situation that is tragic and needs your prayer. You could also pray for the people suffering who you don't know, asking for God's comfort and mercy.

Weed: What was it like to pray for those who are hurting today? Did you see anything sad today? Tell Jesus about the sadness, them pause and imagine the love of God pouring all over you and the sadness.

Friday
......

Till: Jesus, you spent time alone with your Father. How much more do we need that time! Help us to make room to be with you, alone.

Plant: Matthew 14:13-21

Water:

> » Practice it: At the start of this story, Jesus is heading off to be alone, because of the news about John the Baptist's death. Jesus is here practicing solitude, which is the discipline of making time to be alone with God, without any agenda except to be with him. We can seek solitude when our souls are feeling weighed down, or to prepare our hearts, or to teach ourselves to depend on God more than on other people. Today, set aside some time to invite each family member into solitude. A shallow box of sand in which children can draw their thoughts of God can help move them into solitude.

Weed: How was your practice of solitude today? How did it change your day? When did you experience God's presence today?

Saturday

Till: Jesus, you intend for us to walk where you walk. You intend for us to do what you do! Teach us to trust you when you call us beyond our own ability.

Plant: Matthew 14:22-36

Water:

> » Draw it: Draw your favorite scene from this story.

> » Enter it: How do you think Peter felt when he saw Jesus on the water? How do you think it felt to be invited to walk on the water with Jesus?

> » Apply it: Where might Jesus be inviting you to do something that seems impossible? (Examples: Forgiving someone who hurt you, giving up something, serving someone you don't like.) How might you trust him and step out of the boat?

Weed: Did you step out of the boat today? How? Was there a time when you stayed in the boat, afraid? How could you remember God's help next time?

Week of Sunday closest to Nov 9

Sunday

Till: Jesus, help us to follow you when you invite us. Give us wisdom to see through our excuses.

Plant: Luke 14:12-24

Water:

> » List it: In today's parable, Jesus tells about a dinner that many of the invited don't attend. They make excuses. What are some excuses we might make for not responding to God's invitation to live with him in his kingdom?

> » Try it: Rather than offering excuses, try an experiment based on Jesus' teaching. Today he tells us to try serving people who can't repay us, who have nothing to offer in return. Come up with an idea for how to do this, and try it as a family sometime in the next week.

Weed: When did you experience goodness today? What are you most or least grateful for today?

Monday
·······

Till: Jesus, you look at our hearts, not our outward behavior. You're not impressed by empty rule-following. Help us worship you with our hearts as well as with our bodies!

Plant: Matthew 15:1-20

Water:

» Imagine it: Why do you think it is so easy for us to follow rules instead of loving God from the heart?

» Get to the heart of it: What is one practice, rule, or responsibility that you could engage in from your heart today? Try it.

Weed: What was it like to live from your heart instead of just trying to follow the rules? What drew you to God today? What drew you away from God today?

Tuesday
·········

Till: God, you love and bless the outsiders. You love and bless the ones who we think don't deserve your help. Please, give us the same kind of wide-open heart.

Plant: Matthew 15:21-28

Water:

» Act it: Act out this story. What do you learn as you enter into the story?

» Rethink it: In Jesus' day, it seemed obvious that God was for the people of Israel, not for other people. But this woman understood that God has enough love and concern to go around for everyone. Spend some time together rethinking: who might God care about that you tend to think he wouldn't love?

> » Apply it: Who could you treat with love or kindness today that you usually wouldn't?

Weed: When did you get to treat someone with love today? How did it feel? Was there a time when you didn't feel someone deserved to be treated well? Tell God about this, them pause and imagine the love of God pouring all over you and all over the world.

Wednesday

Till: God, you are blazingly alive among us! Help us be on the watch for your life.

Plant: Matthew 15:29-39

Water:

> » Expect it: Jesus' miracles let all the people around him know that God's life and kingdom was right there, among them! Sometimes we don't expect God to be with us. Where could you expect God to be with you today?

> » Live it: How would you act differently in a situation if you knew God was ruling right there? How might you love more courageously?

Weed: Where did you expect God to show up today? Did you see him? Was there any time when you found it hard to feel like God was there?

Thursday

Till: Jesus, help us to keep the bread of our faith free from the yeast of the Pharisees. Let us be more interested in walking with you than in signs and rules.

Plant: Matthew 16:1-12

Water:

- » See it: Jesus scolds the Pharisees for failing to see what's right in front of them: God's life, present in Jesus! Today, go on a walk as a family, even if it's just around the backyard or the block, and point out where you see God's love in ordinary, everyday stuff. Don't overlook the things you see constantly!

- » Praise it: If you have been using Good Dirt for the last year, then as a family you have read the gospels over and over. Take some time to share with one another your favorite things about Jesus. How does Jesus show you what God is like? Turn this into praise!

Weed: How did you see God in everyday stuff today? What do you love about Jesus right now? When did you experience beauty today?

Friday

Till: Jesus, you are the chosen one, the Christ, the Son of the living God! You opened the door to God's kingdom. We praise you!

Plant: Matthew 16:13-20

Water:

- » Say it: Jesus asks the disciples an important question: "Who do you say I am?" God helps Peter to recognize that Jesus is the Son of God. Take some time to let each family member share who they know Jesus to be. How do you see Jesus?

- » Create it: Make a piece of art—a poster, a poem, a sculpture, a song— that proclaims who you say Jesus is. Present it to him as a gift of praise!

Weed: End your day together by enjoying your art project one more time, reminding each other who you say Jesus is.

Saturday

Till: Jesus, we want you to lead us in your way. Help us to follow you, even into self-sacrifice. Help us find our true self in you.

Plant: Matthew 16:21-28

Water:

» Name it: Jesus invites us to let go of control and follow him. Following him means learning not to need to get our own way. We have to learn to trust Jesus and release what we want, so that we are able to do good for others. Can you name some areas in which it's hard not to get what you want?

» Practice it: Pick one of those difficult areas and practice not getting your own way. Let your siblings get the bigger scoop of ice cream. Or, pick the longer line. Allow someone else to play with the toy you love, then try to enjoy their happiness.

Weed: What was it like practicing self-sacrifice today? How does that feel different than needing to get your way? When did you experience generosity today?

Week of Sunday closest to Nov 16

Sunday

Till: God, help us to use our minds to be creative and persistent in doing good for our world. Let hard things spur us on to even more creativity, with you at our side.

Plant: Luke 16:1-13

Water:

» Brainstorm it: Use your creative thinking to come up with an unusual idea for how to bless someone.

» Turn it: What is a difficult or unfair situation that you have to face today? Now, brainstorm again how you can turn it into a chance to do good for someone.

» Live it: Today, be on the lookout for times when you can turn disappointments or frustrations into creative opportunities to love someone! Remember that God is working with you there!

Weed: What was it like looking at disappointments as a chance to do good? What did you do today to be working with God for goodness? When did you experience goodness today?

Monday

Till: Jesus, you are radiant with the power and goodness of God! We worship you!

Plant: Matthew 17:1-13

Water:

> » Draw it: Create a drawing of this wonderful scene!

> » View it: This story is the basis for a very famous icon by Theophanes the Great, "The Transfiguration." Find this picture (it'll show up at once if you Google it) and print it out. Hang it with your drawings of the scene. Spend some time as a family gazing on them, allowing some time of silence.

> » Discuss it: What do these pictures make you feel about Jesus?

Weed: Where did you gaze on Jesus today? As you go to bed tonight, place the pictures someplace you can see them, and gaze on them as you prepare for sleep.

Tuesday

Till: God, help us to take you seriously! We believe, but we need you to help our unbelief.

Plant: Matthew 17:14-21

Water:

> » Remembering it: Jesus invited his disciples to take God seriously. He wants us to really trust that he is with us. He is doing good through us as we live with him. As it was for the disciples, it's sometimes hard for us to remember God! Choose something to help you remember. You could carry a small cross in your pocket, or write a favorite verse on a

card, or put a sticky note on the fridge. Do something to point your heart back to trusting in God, over and over.

Weed: Was your day any different since you were carrying a reminder to trust in God? When was it hard to trust that He was with you? When did you experience the presence of God?

Wednesday
. . . .

Till: God, thank you that we are your children. We are free! Help us to live with joy as your children today.

Plant: Matthew 17:22-27

Water:

» Own it: Jesus teaches us that we are God's children. Today, own that identity! Make a nametag for each member of the family, and write on it, "(Name), child of God!"

» Discuss it: How does it make you feel to know that you are a child of God?

Weed: When did you feel like God's child today? Was it hard to feel like God's child at any point today? Tell this to God, then pause and imagine the love of God pouring out all over you.

Thursday
. . . .

(If today is Thanksgiving, go to page 177.)

Till: Jesus, you truly do love children! God, you don't overlook the little ones! We praise you!

Plant: Matthew 18:1-9

Water:

> » Be it: Today, just enjoy being children! God loves kids, with their silliness and trust and playfulness. Adults, take today to be a little more childlike, too.

Weed: How does it make you feel to know that God loves kids? When did you experience kindness and patience today?

Friday

Till: God, help us to forgive those who harm us. Help us to work out our differences. Even when it's hard, help us to treat those who hurt us with love.

Plant: Matthew 18:10-20

Water:

> » Practice it: How could you take a step today toward forgiving someone who has hurt you? Would it look like treating them nicely? Or, maybe it would look like remembering how much God forgives you?

> » Discuss it: Why is it hard to forgive people who have hurt us? Why do you think God forgives us?

Weed: When were you able to practice forgiveness today? What are you the most and least grateful for today?

Saturday

Till: God, you have forgiven us so much. Help us to follow in your footsteps and forgive others.

Plant: Matthew 18:21-35

Water:

» Act it: Turn today's story into a drama.

» Discuss it: When it's hard to forgive, how does it help to remember God's forgiveness? What are some things you are glad God has forgiven you? Remember that forgiveness happens when we don't wish the person who hurt us any ill will. We hope that God will love them too. Forgiveness is when we let God have the person instead of trying to hold on to them.

Weed: When were you able to practice forgiveness today? What was hard about practicing forgiveness today? Tell God about this, then pause and imagine the love of God pouring all over you.

Thanksgiving Day

Seasonal Fun:

Thanksgiving Day can fall in this week or next, depending on the year. While each family has its own traditions, sometimes we can get so busy with the football game and the food that we forget to take a moment to truly give thanks. Here are some ideas:

» Thanks-giving Basket: As your table centerpiece, create a basket of thanks. Have each person write on a card some things they thank God for. Then at dinner, have each person pull out someone else's card and read it.

» Overflow your thanks: Many families use Thanksgiving as a time to show their gratitude by helping those in need. Most food pantries and homeless shelters are in need of donations of Thanksgiving dinner food—especially frozen turkeys! Some will even allow your family to make a delivery to a family in need. Call around and see how your family can help.

» Give thanks for one another: Take the opportunity to bless one another by giving thanks. One by one, go around the table and allow each family member to share why you are thankful for this person.

» Welcome others to the table: Thanksgiving is a day for family, but there are lots of people who don't have anyone to share it with. In your own church and workplace there are probably singles, widows, single parents, and college students who don't have anywhere to go. Who could you invite to share this day with your family?

Till: We give thanks to you, God, for all the wonderful gifts you give us: family, friends, life, and everything we need. You are the source of all our blessings. Thank you!

Plant: Matthew 6:25-33

Water:

» Celebrate it: The discipline of Celebration is serious business! We need to recall God's goodness, and put down the hardships of life, so that we remember that we live in God's abundance. Today put a pause on thinking about the things that are stressful. Release the pressure for dinner to be perfect, or for everyone to get along without issues. Just accept today, and celebrate, no matter where you are in life.

Weed: When did you give or receive love today? When did you experience faithfulness today?

Week of Sunday closest to Nov 23

Christ the King Sunday

Till: Jesus, this is your kingdom, and you are the king! Rule over our lives today. We celebrate your rule, your power, and your kingdom!

Plant: John 18:33-37

Water:

» Crown it: This is the last Sunday of the church year, and we turn our hearts to the King of the kingdom—Jesus! Soon it will be time to pull out the Advent decorations and start the cycle again. Today, pause and "crown the year" with praise! Ask:

  » Where have you seen God at work this year?

  » How have you seen God change you this year?

  » Where have you seen Christ as King this year?

  » Share with your children how you have seen them grow into the kingdom this year. Don't miss this chance to bless them!

» Create it: Let every family member do an art project celebrating the reign of Jesus, such as a picture, a poem, a song, or a dance. Share your art in praise of the King!

Weed: What gave you joy or sorrow today? When did you experience the presence of God?

Monday
· · · · · · · ·

Till: God, you gave us marriage to help us understand that you love us without end. You never let us go! Help us to love like you do.

Plant: Matthew 19:1-12

Water:

>> Discuss it: This passage opens a good opportunity to talk about marriage. Depending on the circumstances of your home, this conversation can go in a lot of ways. It's important for kids to gain an understanding that God's love is eternal, and his commitment never ends. Talk about this as a family today.

Weed: How does it feel to know that God will never, ever let you go? What drew you to God today? What drew you away from God today?

Tuesday
· · · · · · · ·

Till: God, sometimes we think you just want us to follow the rules, but you want our whole heart and our whole life! Help us give everything to you.

Plant: Matthew 19:13-22

Water:

>> List it: What are some of the rules you think God wants you to keep? Why does Jesus seem to think that these rules aren't the point? Could you keep these rules and not love God?

» Imagine it: Reread the story, imagining yourself as the ruler. What are the things you tell Jesus that you've done well? What does Jesus invite you to let go of? Give some time for each family member to think and respond.

Weed: When did you go past the rules today to really love God and people? When did you experience kindness today?

Wednesday
....

Till: So many things look impossible to us, God. We can trust you to help us! Let us learn to trust you more and more each day.

Plant: Matthew 19:23-30

Water:

» Draw it: Jesus uses a silly picture, but it helps us get an idea of how impossible it is to live in God's kingdom on our own strength. Draw your best version of a camel trying to run through the eye of a needle.

» Rest it: Since it's so impossible for us to do kingdom life on our own, today practice resting in God. When you feel anxious or afraid of something that seems difficult, take an extra moment to put the issue on God's shoulders. Try praying something like "God, I know you've got this. Help me rest."

Weed: How did it feel to put your stresses on God's shoulders? When did you try to live on your own today? When did you experience the presence of God today?

Thursday
· · · · · · · · ·

(If today is Thanksgiving, go to page 177.)

Till: God, you are generous to everyone. You are generous even to those we don't think deserve it! Help us to rejoice in your generosity, instead of being stingy.

Plant: Matthew 20:1-16

Water:

> » Act it: Turn this story into a drama. Take turns being the first and the last workers.

> » Reverse it: Today, live in the upside-down kingdom. Let the youngest be first, and the oldest be last. Give generously to everybody, even if they haven't been nice.

Weed: How was it living in the upside-down kingdom today? Are you glad God is generous, or would you rather He treat everyone equally? Tell God about this, then pause and imagine the love of God pouring all over you.

Friday
· · · · · ·

Till: So often we just want to push our way to the front, Jesus. We forget how much those in charge have to suffer in order to love others. Help us to become servants wherever we are.

Plant: Matthew 20:17-28

Water:

> » Serve it: Look for opportunities to be a servant. Instead of pushing to get what you want, keep your eyes open for times you can help others get what they need.

» Accept it: Part of being a servant is learning not to complain. Schedule a 24-hour fast from complaining. That means everybody—adults, too!

Weed: What was it like to be a servant? When were you able to serve? What is hard about being a servant? How can you share that with God?

Saturday

Till: Jesus, it is so good to know that our hurts and disappointments matter to you. Thank you for being compassionate! Thank you for healing us!

Plant: Matthew 20:29-34

Water:

» Ask it: Today, we see how Jesus responds to our hurts. He is deeply moved! He wants to help! If there is a hurt in your life, share that with Jesus today. You might ask for his help aloud, or write him a letter, or draw him a picture expressing how you feel.

» See it: The crowd in the story tried to hush up the blind men instead of helping them get to Jesus. Practice bringing other people's hurts to Jesus today. You might keep your eyes open for hurting people, and pray silently for them; or, you might get the newspaper as a family, and pray for the people in stories that touch your heart. Bring these people's concerns to Jesus, just as you brought your own.

Weed: How did it feel to bring your hurts to Jesus? How did it feel to bring other people's hurts to Jesus? Tell Jesus about these hurts, then pause and imagine the love of God pouring out all over you.

CHURCH YEAR CALENDAR

....

Year	Advent	Lent	Holy Week	Easter	Pentecost
2013-14	Dec 1	March 5	April 13	April 20	June 8
2014-15	Nov 30	Feb 18	March 29	April 5	May 24
2015-16	Nov 29	Feb 10	March 20	March 27	May 15
2016-17	Nov 27	March 1	April 9	April 16	June 4
2017-18	Dec 3	Feb 14	March 25	April 1	May 20
2018-19	Dec 2	March 6	April 14	April 21	June 9
2019-20	Dec 1	Feb 26	April 5	April 12	May 31
2020-21	Nov 29	Feb 17	March 28	April 4	May 23
2021-22	Nov 28	March 2	April 10	April 17	June 5
2022-23	Nov 27	Feb 22	April 2	April 9	May 28
2023-24	Dec 3	Feb 14	March 24	March 31	May 19
2024-25	Dec 1	March 5	April 13	April 20	June 8
2025-26	Nov 30	Feb 18	March 29	April 5	May 24
2026-27	Nov 29	Feb 10	March 21	March 28	May 16
2027-28	Nov 28	March 1	April 9	April 16	June 4
2028-29	Dec 3	Feb 14	March 25	April 1	May 27

CONTRIBUTORS

Lacy Finn Borgo

Lacy Finn Borgo writes for the spiritual formation of children because she has children and she likes them. She has a Master's Degree in Education from the State University of New York Geneseo and has taught in both public and private schools in Texas, New York, Colorado, and Kazakhstan. Lacy is a graduate of the Renovaré Institute for Spiritual Formation. She is the author of *Life with God for Children: Engaging Biblical Stories and Practices for Spiritual Formation* released by Renovaré. Lacy has written three picture books—*Big Mama's Baby, Day and Night,* and *The Mighty Hurricane.* Lacy lives in Colorado where she tends both the physical and spiritual gardens of her family.

Ben Barczi

Ben Barczi serves as Pastor of Spiritual Formation at First Baptist Church in San Luis Obispo, California. He is a graduate of California Polytechnic in San Luis Obispo, where he studied Philosophy, and a graduate of the Renovaré Institute for Spiritual Formation. Ben loves teaching about spiritual formation, and enjoys living a semi-monastic life ordered by the rhythms of Daily Prayer, regular solitude, and good conversations at amazing local coffeeshops.

Made in the USA
Middletown, DE
19 February 2021